A guide to
basket weaving

MARIE PIERONI

Schiffer
Publishing Ltd

4880 Lower Valley Road • Atglen, PA 19310

Published by Schiffer Publishing, Ltd.
4880 Lower Valley Road
Atglen, PA 19310
Phone: (610) 593-1777; Fax: (610) 593-2002
E-mail: Info@schifferbooks.com

For our complete selection of fine books on this and related subjects, please visit our website at www.schifferbooks.com. You may also write for a free catalog.

This book may be purchased from the publisher. Please try your bookstore first.

We are always looking for people to write books on new and related subjects. If you have an idea for a book, please contact us at proposals@schifferbooks.com

Schiffer Publishing's titles are available at special discounts for bulk purchases for sales promotions or premiums. Special editions, including personalized covers, corporate imprints, and excerpts can be created in large quantities for special needs. For more information, contact the publisher.

Library of Congress Control Number: 2014939588

ISBN: 978-0-7643-4530-2
Printed in China

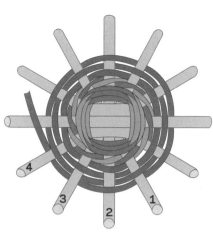
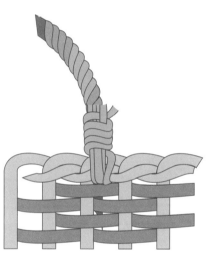

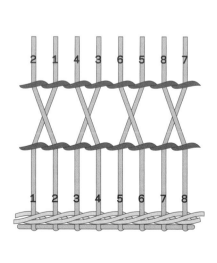

Contents

Basics

In this first chapter we will take you on a short journey to discover basket weaving: its history, its vocabulary, its different forms, its raw materials and its tools.

Introduction

Since the dawn of time basket weaving has been an integral part of human activities — agricultural, domestic or commercial.

It is certainly because of this familiarity that for a long time basket weaving wasn't entirely considered as a part of the arts and crafts circle. Nevertheless, the authenticity of its materials, the wealth of its technique, its discreet robustness and its natural beauty are all qualities that make it irreplaceable, today more than ever.

Basket weaving is one of the most ancient human activities. Although ancient vegetable fibers have degraded to a point where only rare fragments have been found, fossilized traces have shown that this activity has been practiced for several thousand years. Many paleontologists believe that basket weaving pre-dates the invention of terracotta because certain relics suggest that early examples of pottery were poured into moulds made of woven grass.

In times when it was vital to preserve and transport utensils and foodstuff, basket weaving played an important role, as vegetation, found everywhere, was easier to work with than animal hide. Egyptian and Celtic civilizations wove containers thick enough to hold water; they also wove roofs, walls, fences, and even parts of their clothing.

Even before basket weaving became an established art it showed our ancestors' capacity to use natural resources to fit their immediate needs. You only need to watch a child playing in a garden to see how he spontaneously tries to create objects by braiding twigs, daisies and grass.

Long before corporations came into existence during the Middle-Ages, baskets had been a part of everyone's lives, filling the needs of the agricultural, commercial, or domestic world. In the long months between harvest and planting, baskets were woven by workmen, peasants, shepherds and fishermen, even made by the oldest or youngest members of the family. Many itinerant workers found a source of income through basket weaving: they made simple articles by using raw materials cut from roadside hedges and their wares found immediate success among house-wives and merchants alike.

A weaving tradition grew among these wandering workers and all used a common weave, but because they frequently moved from place to place, new and interesting techniques were born. Little by little these "sieve-makers" settled in one village or another and became real masters of their craft renowned throughout the region. Usually settling down in an area where willows grew in abundance, they also developed "willow culture." The 19th century saw the rise of workshops and factories producing woven items, along with many other activities. It was an era when craftsmen were solicited for huge orders of standardized goods: from fisheries to demi-

johns, from bouquets to luxury confectionaries — nothing was sold without a wicker packaging.

At the end of the 19th century packages made of wicker gave way to wood fiber products such as cardboard and later to plastic materiel; it was the same for furniture and other domestic accessories where new materials became the "in" thing of modern times. Items made of cane, raffia and straw where shuffled off the market without even being considered made from ancient, noble materials.

Nevertheless, basketwork has shown itself to be irreplaceable for a great number of items and is still a part of our everyday lives, even in commercial and industrial fields. Being both lightweight and robust it is a favorite item used for stands displaying bread, fruit, linen, wool and fragile objects in markets, small stores and supermarkets. It is also used for occasional and garden furniture and for the baskets that hang below hot-air balloons!

Today, thanks to people looking for authentic and aesthetic, practical and ecological qualities, basketwork is once again becoming an important item in our homes. Several companies have worked hard to ensure that it has its place in the arts and crafts world through expositions of traditional and modern wicker-work.

Knowing about basket weaving helps us to understand and appreciate these items when we buy them in markets and stores. The techniques used to create them vary according to the materials used and also to the traditions that are intimately linked to the region where they were made. So the common point between an oyster basket made out of rush by a fisherman, a basket of hedge-row twigs made by an itinerant worker, or an Asian vase made of tiny slivers of bamboo, is the ingenuity of

each craftsman to use the raw materials he had to hand, to create an object that answered a specific need.

If this knowledge is useful when it comes to appreciating recently made items, for aficionados the real pleasure comes from recognizing ancient articles they find in antique markets and yard sales: items that seem to transport you back in time to an era when they were prized and expensive, back to a time when their makers worked hard to create them for a specific use.

Their very names evoke a long-forgotten way of life; some of them speak for themselves: the grape-pickers and gleaners basket, or the Sunday picnic basket opened on a river-bank; the sailor's basket that held his neatly packed uniform, without forgetting the bulrush basket that carried Moses along the Nile, which gave birth to the wicker-work basinets and prams, which rocked and transported children for many generations.

Other delicious names given to shopping baskets showed how important they were in everyday life: Lucette, mandelette, Tosca, marlier, timbale (from the Lorraine or Picardy areas), chaloupe, gondola, crocane bouju, etc. Learning basket weaving offers you the chance to practice a generous craft. It allows you to create beautiful, practical and long-lasting objects from a few strands of vegetation. You only need to take the time to understand and repeat the simple gestures that are rich in ancient skill, to discover for yourself the pleasure of creating something from natural materials. You will give life to your own unique pieces of work that match your taste and your needs, and which will accompany you faithfully for many years.

VOCABULARY

Banneton. Basket where dough rose. By extension, a bread basket.

Cloyère. A long basket without a handle, either closed-weave or ribbed, without handles used to carry up to twenty five dozen oysters

Crocane. Closed-weave basket with a large handle. Crocane is a weaving technique.

Flein. Small open-weave basket used for the transportation and preservation of fragile fruit.

Lucette. Closed-weave shopping basket, either round or oval with a large handle.

Manne. Large storage basket with two small handles.

Pique-nique. A slim closed-weave rectangular picnic basket.

Timbale. A full closed-weave basket with a more or less convex lid and a small handle

Raw materials

For a long time woven items were created using vegetation that men found close to their homes.

The resulting large diversity was further enriched over the years thanks to the selection of species and the importation of exotic plants. Among all this material, each with its own quality and charm, it is important to know how to choose the right matter adapted to the type of object you wish to create and to your ability.

BASKET WILLOW (OSIER)

This is without doubt the preferential material in traditional basket weaving, because it grows wild on moist ground around the world. It was harvested from along riverbanks and used to weave baskets for domestic and agricultural purposes. In Europe, little by little, willow plantations were created, often cultivated by basket makers. These plantations meant that the best species were selected and productivity increased. Although professional willow culture considerably regressed during the 20th century, it is still very much alive in the few regions where basket weaving is still practiced.

Osier is a willow belonging to the salicaceae family (Salix). There are a number of varieties of willow and the most frequently used are S.viminalis and S. triandra for their smooth aspect; S. alba-vittelina which is supple and good for rib-basket weaving, S. purpurea daphnoïde for its reddish color, and S. Americana, princi-

pally kept for making splints. Basket willows have ligneous stems, which in spring produce catkins and later leaves. It is advisable to plant them in regular rows, in moist but well-drained, weed-free soil. Every winter before the sap rises, the shoots are cut, except for those left to grow for two or three years to obtain thicker stems. The stumps can live for many decades.

Willow stems (called strands) measure between 2 and 10 feet. The longer they are, the thicker the foot is. When they are green (freshly cut) they aren't good for use in basket weaving as they retract as they dry out. Willow comes in three categories, according to the type of preparation used:

Raw willow. Also called "brown willow," it hasn't been treated in any way apart from drying out for several months.

While drying its bark takes on a brown hue, which varies in intensity depending on the variety of the bush.

White willow. Cut while the sap is rising (in spring), white willow is immediately stripped of its bark with the help of a peeler or a decortications machine. To make peeling easier, the bases of the strands are generally stood in tanks of water. Then they are peeled and placed outside to dry in the sun, which whitens them.

Buff willow. Cut before the sap rises, the strands are left to dry out, before being plunged into boiling water and being stripped of their bark. They are then dried again. Their reddish color comes from the tannin which dissolves in the boiling water. Strands several centimeters in diameter are often stripped this way.

Willow strands can be divided into equal stakes using a Boxwood cleave or with a machine. It is also possible to shave off the sapwood in splints.

Whichever manner is used to prepare them, willow strands always present a decreasing diameter from the base to the top. This means that they need to be correctly positioned to keep your work even. Because willow is robust you will be able to create objects both dense and solid in well defined forms. On the other hand, its rigidity leaves little room for error, because once woven, the willow is marked with a fold which deforms it irreparably.

You can keep a stock of willow for several years, as long as it is kept in a dry, well-aired place out of direct sunlight. Before use, willow strands need to be made supple by soaking (see page 17).

RATTAN

Imported into Europe since the 15th century, rattan has as important a place in basket weaving as willow, although it plays a somewhat different role. It offers a wider range of possibilities, thanks to the large diversity of its natural thickness as well as its possibility to be graded, curved and tinted. At the same time more robust and suppler than willow, it is good for creating strong, utilitarian items, furniture and fancy pieces of fine art. It is the raw material the most used by amateur weavers, especially beginners.

Rattan comes from a vine-like plant of the palm family (genus Calamus); both creeping and climbing it can reach several hundred feet in length. It grows wild in various equatorial or tropical forests, mainly in south-east Asia, where each variety bears the name of the region where it is gathered. Once stripped of the silica that covers it and the leaves, the core rattan is washed and left to dry out.

Raw rattan. Diameters vary from 2 millimeters (Pulut rattan) to more than 2 inches (Manau rattan).

Peeled rattan. The diameter is at least 1.5 centimeters which has been decorticated and polished for use in the fabrication of feet and sides of furniture and which can be varnished.

Spun rattan. This regroups all the material made by machining rattan with a die.

The round core is obtained by dividing the interior of the rattan into cylindrical stems graded from 1.5mm to 2cm.

The leaves are fine bands from 5 to 7 mm wide cut on the perimeter of the vine and whose brightness is called "enamel"; they are called "settled" when their edges have been mechanically planed.

The cane is a flat strand of between 1.5 and 4mm wide, which still bears its bark. It is also used for caning chairs.

The splint of core is cut from the interior of the rattan.

In all its forms, rattan is very pale yellow in color. Heavier and more resistant than willow, it is also easier to work because of its flexibility and its regular diameter. The fine core is used for decorative work and small objects. Before use rattan has to be soaked, the time varies depending on the thickness of the strands. (See page 17).

BAMBOO

Although this plant, which is a member of the gramineae family, grows in diverse climates, European basket weavers rarely use it. Being hollow it is impossible to bend, therefore it is only exploitable for stakes, corner poles, extra bases (it is more resistant than wood) or used in the form of fine splints. The latter needs special techniques, perfectly mastered by Asian craftsmen.

RUSH, GRASS AND STRAW

In basket weaving these fibers are reserved for light baskets, fancy accessories, hats, finishes or ornamental details. Their use and their names vary from region to region.

Rushes and reeds grow in water. The maritime rush has more solid strands and it is possible to use it either as it is or braided (usually consisting of three plaited strands).

Particularly fine fibers, such as straw, rye, marsh grass or raffia, are generally braided into cords of a few millimeters in diameter. Another process — closer to the esparto method — consists of rolling the fibers in spirals, assembled and kept in place par small cane ties. Even when they are braided, the flexibility of all these fibers necessitates working around a form (see page 52).

TREE BRANCHES

In certain regions of Europe where woods are naturally more abundant than willow, basket weaving traditions have developed around working with tree branches. These provide ribs, moulds, and the stakes as well as partitions less flexible than willow, but just as solid.

The branches mainly come from chestnut and hazel trees and blackberry bushes. Climbing plants (black alder, honeysuckle, clematis, etc.) provide finer, suppler stems.

Baskets woven in wood have their own rustic charm. Don't forget that gathering wild materials should be done with respect for Nature and in accordance with the laws that protect the environment.

DIVERSE MATERIAL

The stakes used in basket-work need solidity that only willow, rattan, and wood can offer. On the other hand if you are more interested in creativity than solidity, you can do the filling-in with almost any fiber: raffia, synthetic fibers, twine, ribbon, cord, wire, paper strands, etc.

Choosing the right material

First and foremost, the choice of the material should be compatible with the function and style of the object; however so that working is a pleasure and the results pleasing, take working conditions and your own capacities into account. For example, soaking willow, if you live in a small house, could prove difficult; bending a thick mould needs a certain strength; manipulation of fine splint or core requires patience and dexterity.

Note

If they are treated properly, basketry objects — especially those made of willow and rattan — will remain beautiful and solid for many decades.

Preparation

The different types of material should be kept dry, in bales for the thickest, in hanks for the finest. On the other hand, tree branches must be kept moist throughout the work, but without being water-logged: if they are too wet they will deform the object when they dry out and will turn black or will rot. Before using them, plunge them into clear water (soaking), then for some, preserve them in a regularly dampened cloth and covered with a plastic cover (sweating).

Depending on the size of the strands, soak them in a bowl, the bath, or a large tank; using hot water will lessen the soaking time. Use a weight of some sort to keep the strands under water.

Sometimes it is necessary to run a part of the work under water or to soak it for a few minutes to make it supple again.

Coloring and upkeep

Before weaving the strands, you can soak them in a dye bath. This way you can play around with colors. You can also dye, varnish, or paint the finished object. An air-brush will give better results than a traditional paint brush, because it will get into all the cracks.

Choose colors made especially for wood or use natural products, like walnut stain. Dust your woven items regularly. To clean them, use a nylon brush dipped in a solution of warm water and bicarbonate of soda (one teaspoon per quart of water). If they have turned grey, use lemon juice or hydrogen peroxide (four teaspoons per quart of water) in cold water. You can find in any DIY store colorless varnish which will protect basketwork from stains and water.

MATERIAL	PREPARATION AND PERIOD OF USE
Raw willow	Soaking: 8/10 days. Use: a few days. Avoid re-soaking.
White willow Buff willow	Soaking: 2/6 hours. Use: a few hours Sweating: a few hours, then while working. Avoid re-soaking.
Raw rattan	Soaking: 2/4 days. Use: a few days
Spun rattan	Soaking: 10/30 minutes. Use: a few days Sweating: during work. Re-soak if necessary.
Rush	Mist just before use. Sweating: during work, 4 hours maximum.
Straw Ropes of grass	Soaking: 5/30 minutes; leave it to drain. Use: a few hours.
Tree branches	Use before they have dried out, without misting them.

Tools

The basic tools used in basket weaving are rudimentary and haven't changed much in spite of technical progress. You can find them in any arts-and-crafts store or in hardware stores.

Basic equipment

PEELER

Used for peeling the objects, taking off any protruding pieces. Alternatively, you can use pruners (1) or cutting pliers.

WEAVER'S PRUNING KNIFE (2)

Its curved blade is perfectly adapted for splitting strands, regardless of the cut desired (see page 23).

RAPPING IRON (3)

This is a rectangular metal tongue used to tap the weave at the end of each row to pack it down. The ring handle is useful for straightening large strands. If you can't find this item, you can replace it with a packing-and-tucking tool.

AWL (4)

Straight or curved, an awl is useful for making spaces or holes in the weave so that it is easier to insert stakes. The size of the awl should be adapted to the size of the material used.

NEEDLE NOSE PLIERS (5)

Used for bending stakes.

REED GAUGE

This item is used to measure the diameter of the strands. You can find them with crenels adapted to measuring rattan core (6) and willow strands (7).

Make sure that you have twine for temporary tying, and a tape measure so that you can keep an eye on the length and width of your work. Don't forget to put something heavy (8), on the base of your object, to stabilize it while you are working. If you have a heavy piece of wood, it is easy to fix it to the base using a bolt with a wingnut in the center.

Shaping square or rectangular objects is done with a die (see page 52). For this you need two wooden poles, a hammer and nails. If you are using a ready-made wooden base, add a saw, gimlets in varying diameters or a drill. Many arts-and-crafts stores sell ready-made wooden bases. To make a round or oval base on a mould, you need a board of at least 5mm thick, slightly larger than the desired size. Using a small blowtorch will make bending rattan easier. Moulds and frames are assembled with tacks that are pressed in with flat nose pliers.

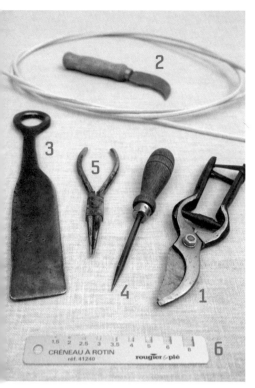

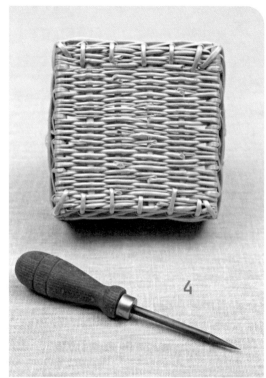

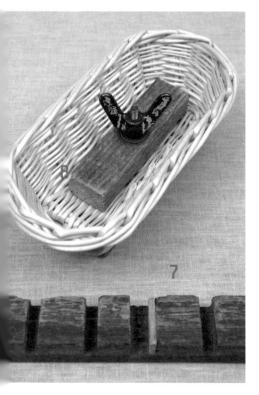

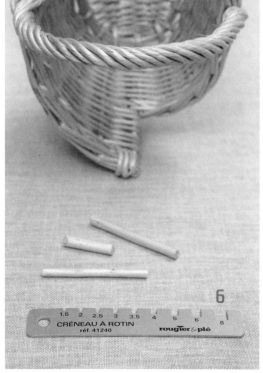

Tools for preparing the material

SPLITTING BRAKE

A long wooden or metal clip through which are passed crude Wicker strands one by one in order to split them.

CLEAVER

This hard wood-handled tool with a brass splitter splits a strand of willow along its length into three or four segments of equal diameters, according to the number of fins that the tool has. Split willow can be used as is or reduced to ribs.

SHAVES

It comes in planes, of which there are two models. One is used to reduce the thickness of the split wicker, the other reduces the width

Advice

When preparing your material, try to get hold of traditional tools, which you will find in specialized arts and crafts or antique stores.

Installation and working position

The working position is very important, because it influences the dexterity with which you manipulate the basketwork through to its realization, and, thus, the quality of the work. Traditionally, the basket maker works sitting on a low stool or on a board on the ground, where he can position the basket at different angles depending on his task. In the course of weaving, the object can be balanced on his knees or on a stool placed between his legs. This position avoids being hindered by a table. It also means that the object can be turned around and tools are within easy reach beside him.

Settle down in a clear space to avoid hurting somebody or knocking anything over while you are manipulating the strands of material. If you are working inside, the floor should be tiled; if not put down a plastic cover to protect the floor from damp material.

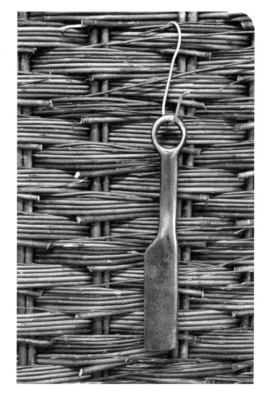

Basketwork structures

With the exception of ribbed baskets, all basketwork objects have an identical structure, whatever their form and the material used. Each object has a base around which the strands are raised. At the bottom of the basket sides, where the strands turn upwards (are upsett), the basket is reinforced by a three strand wale. For closed-weave basketry, the walls are made by interlacing weavers that hide the strands. In open-weave basketry the strands are simply held in place at regular intervals by waling on one or two levels. The object is finished with a border and is then ready for a handle, a lid, fastening accessories or perhaps a foot added to the curved wale to raise the base.

1   Foot
2   Bottom
3   Upsett
4   Closing
5   Height of neck
6   Track
7   Border
8   Handle

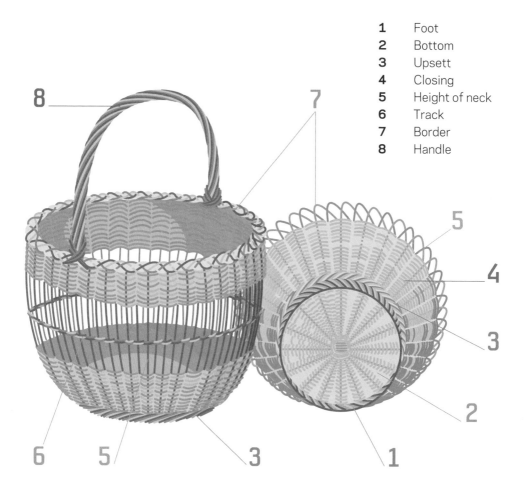

Essential Techniques

Basketwork is an art of experience based on elementary techniques. By getting to know them, you will achieve satisfying results. All the specific terms are explained in the glossary on page 92.

Selecting the material

Choose the weavers according to the size and type of work. Then choose slightly thicker strands for the curved rim and the wale, then even thicker strands for the spokes. Rattan core grading makes this task easier. If you are working with tree branches, sort them into thickness before starting to work. Prepare the material (see page 17).

Splitting

Spokes and weavers should be thinned a little to avoid over-thickness; working with moulds or frames means making various kinds of splits (see next page).

Weaving

Don't re-cut the weavers once you have chosen them. Weave them with a firm but supple gesture. From time to time use the rapping iron and tap the weavers between each spoke to pack them together. When you reach the end of a weaver, be careful when replacing it; if you are working with willow make sure to introduce the weaver the right way, by the foot or by the top (see page 33). If you are a beginner, markers (push-pins or tape) placed at the ends of the weavers and on the basketry will help you understand the progress of the work.

Different types of splitting

Thinning. A cut made in the first centimeters at the end of the weaver to make introducing it easier.

Flat cut. This for fixing, by rolling, to a wooden frame or between two cuts of spoke.

heel

Heel cut. It is preceded by thinning. Its length is equal to the circumference of the edge, the mould, or the framework around which it must fit.

Scarfing Beveling at joining ends of the strands so they can be mated without changing the diameter.

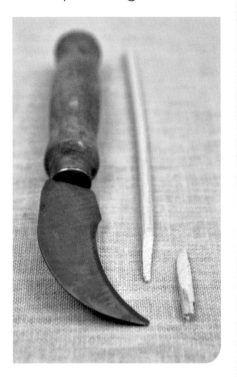

Peeling

At different stages of weaving, it is necessary to "peel" your work; this means cutting off the sticking-out weavers. This can be done with a picking knife, a pruning knife or pruners. An extremity should always be cut obliquely behind a spoke or, if its thickness allows, tucked into the previous level, and cut on the inside.

Correcting mistakes

If you make a mistake, cut the badly placed weavers, remove them and start again with new ones. Even if you re-moisten a used weaver it will stay bent, especially if you are using willow.

Closed-weave basketwork

This type of basketwork is the most wide-spread. Closely interlaced around the spokes, which they hide completely, the weavers compose a dense weave whose aspect varies according to the weaver used.

The base

This is an essential element, because it assures the basket's stability. The technique used varies according to the form and solidity that you want your basket to have.

Round base slath

The slath

From the strands chosen for this use (see page 22), cut six spokes slightly longer than the diameter desired for the base. Using a pruning knife, make a cut in the center of three of the spokes. Do this carefully to avoid splitting the spokes all the way along. Then feed the other three spokes through to form a cross. **(1)** You now have 4 "branches."

The ligature

Choose two long weavers and thin them (see page 23). Tuck their ends side by side into the slit spokes. Pass the weaver A under the first branch of the slath, then place it over the second branch **(2)**

Place the weaver B on the first branch of the slath then under the second **(3)**.

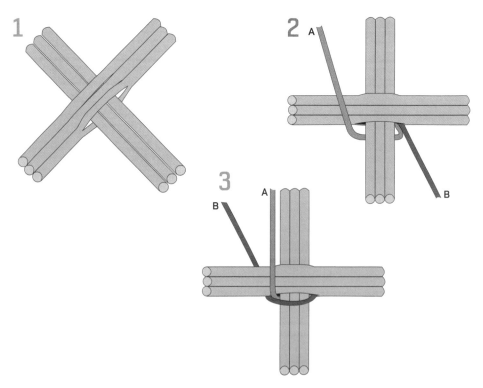

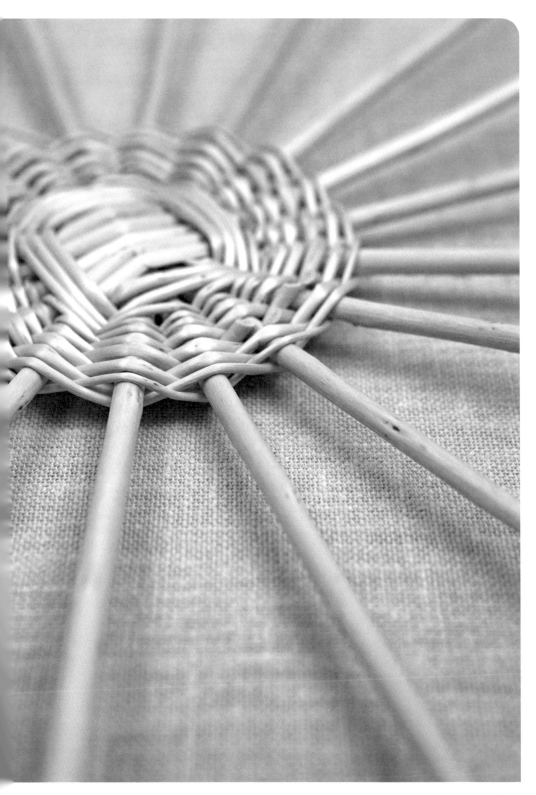

Pass weaver B over weaver A and place it onto the third branch and then under the fourth **(4)**.

Pass weaver A under the third branch, over the fourth and place it alongside the first branch, to the left of weaver B **(5)**. You have now finished the first round of the ligature.

Make sure that the four branches are at right angles and adjust them if necessary. Check on the position of the two weavers: they should closely surround the branches but should be flexible, without overlapping on either of the two sides or being over-thick on the corners. Do two more rounds in the same way as the first. You can hold the slath in any way that feels comfortable, but make sure you always work in the same direction, preferably in a clockwise direction. Pack in the three rounds close to the center of the slath **(6)**.

SCANDINAVIAN SLATH

This version is kept for fine and supple material. The slath is made up of 8 split spokes, entwined to form a motive like a checkerboard. The ligature, breaking out and filling are carried out in the same way as a classical round base.

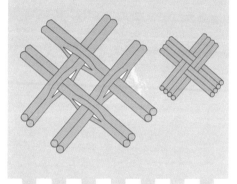

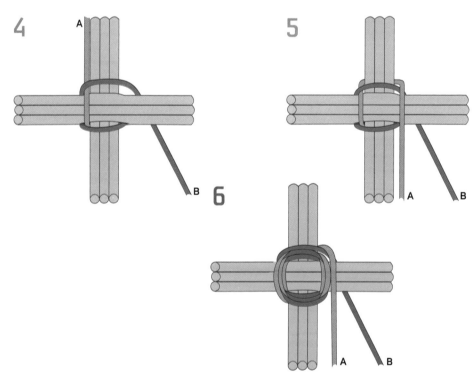

Breaking out (pairing)

Bend the two spokes situated on the exterior of each branch at an angle, to form a star **(1)**.

Using the pairing technique, pass weaver B over weaver A, over the first spoke, under the second and then bring it up **(2)**.

Pass weaver A under the first spoke, over the second, under the third and bring it up **(3)**.

Pass weaver B over the third spoke and weaver A, under the fourth spoke and then bring it up. Finish the round in the same way. Cut the two weavers in a way so that their extremities are on the back of the base **(4)**.

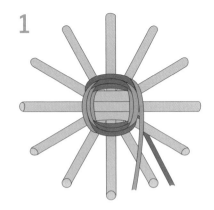

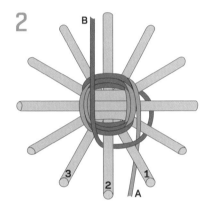

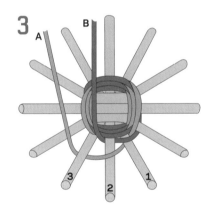

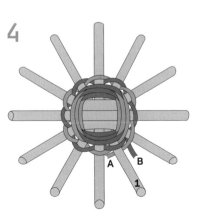

Note

Unless you want to make a flat object (table mat, place mat, tray), a base should be slightly convex so that it will support the pressure of the stakes which will be placed later. To do this, as soon as you have finished the breaking out round and during the filling work, press the sticks down lightly with your fingers at each passage.

Filling

There are four methods of filling. In all the cases, work with weavers that identical to those you used for the ligature and breaking out. See page 33 to learn how to introduce weavers during the course of the work.

PAIRING

Continue to work the same way as for breaking out. The result won't be very elegant, but it will be solid.

FRENCH RANDING (1)

This is the most dense and regular method. You will need as many weavers as you have spokes (twelve for a classical slath). If you calculate their length correctly, you won't need to splice them during the work.

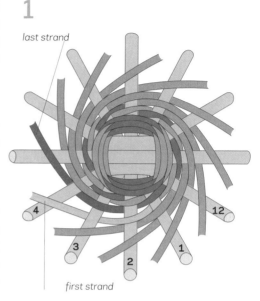

last strand

first strand

Introduce the first weaver under spoke one. Pass it over spoke two, under spoke three then bring it up between spokes three and four. Don't pack it in against the slath because you need the space for the last weaver. Introduce a second weaver under spoke twelve. Pass it over spoke one, under spoke two and then bring it up between spokes two and three. Pack it in close to the first weaver, but keep the space between this and the slath.

In this way, place a weaver under each spoke. Introduce the last weaver under spoke number two by sliding it under weaver number one.

The rest of the rounds follow the order in which you have introduced them at the beginning. Pass each one of them in front of and behind a spoke and then bring it back to the top. Don't forget to pack the rows in from time to time.

Finish by a round of pairing (as in breaking out).

ONE-STRAND SLEW

This is the easiest method: A single weaver passed alternatively over and under the spokes **(2)**. For this you must have an odd number of spokes. To obtain this, split a spoke in two **(3)** or add one during a breaking out round. Another solution is to keep the even number of spokes and then passing the weaver under spokes one and two at the end of the first round, then under spokes two and three at the end of the second round, and so forth **(4)**.

TWO (OR MORE) STRAND SLEW

This is the quickest way. It is the same as one-strand slewing, but using two or more weavers side by side **(5)**.

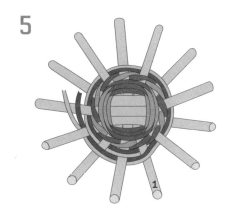

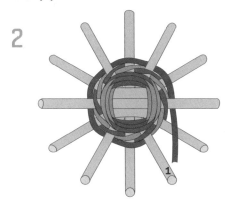

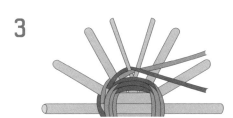

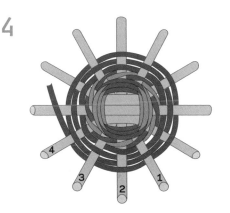

Peeling and size

Peel the bottom (see page 23). Using pruners, cut the spokes flush to the weavers to get the desired diameter.

Base wider than 20 cm

The number of spokes used depends on the diameter of the base: the wider it is, the more spokes are needed to make sure that the weave doesn't collapse. As soon as you think the spokes are too far apart, double their number by inserting a new spoke between each of them **(1)**.

A second solution consists of making a slath with eight or ten strands **(2)**. After a classic ligature, breaking out is done on two rounds: the first separates them two by two **(3)**, the second one by one **(4)**. If a base is visible (a tray for example) you can add a decorative aspect by doing several rounds on two spokes, then a round of three-strand wale (see pages 48-49) on each spoke, then going back to your original weave.

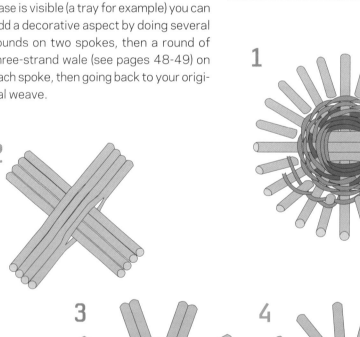

Introducing or replacing a weaver

It is better that the weaver extremities are on the inside or underneath the object. They should be as discrete as possible, for aesthetic reasons and for solidity. To avoid over-thickness, you need to thin down (see page 23) the weavers at the beginning or during the course of the work and to cut them obliquely during peeling.

Don't wait until you get to the end of a weaver before replacing it because a short end will be too difficult to bend into the inside of the work. When there are only a few centimeters left, place the weaver inside the work behind another weaver or a spoke. Place the end of new weaver under the old one, behind the same weaver or spoke. Bring out the new weaver in the same place where the old one would have come out. **(1 & 2)**.

Leave a long enough end on both the old end new weavers on the inside of the work to stop them from slipping out. Cut thcm later during peeling.

The decreasing diameter of the weavers requires planning their replacement all around the work. The rule consists in working from base to top when using a single stalk, and to join base to base or top to top when working with several. In the second case, make a few passes by weaving at the same time the top of the former stalk and that of the new **(3)**.

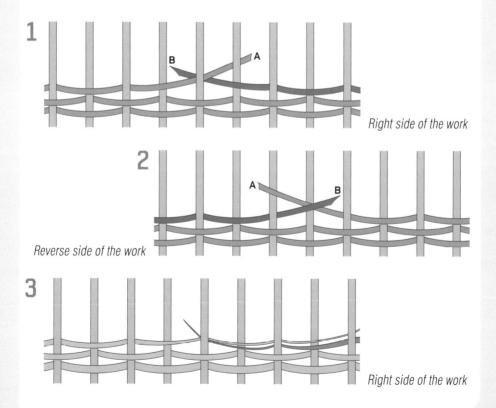

1

B   A

Right side of the work

2

A   B

Reverse side of the work

3

Right side of the work

Oval base slath

The slath

From the chosen strands (see page 22) cut three long ones (length = length of the base + about 5cm) and a series of shorter ones (length= width of the base + about 5cm). The number of side-spokes is proportional to the length of the work, but should not be less than six, which is sufficient for a base of 1 to 1 1/4 feet.

With the pruning knife make a cut in the center of the side-spokes. Do this carefully to avoid splitting them all the way along. Feed in the long spokes. Near each end of the long spokes join two side-spokes and spread the others between them at regular intervals **(1)**, so that the lengths XY and YZ are equal **(2)**.

Ligature

Choose four long weavers and thin the ends (see page 23). Introduce two of them into the split in spoke 3.

Pass the weaver A under the side-spoke 4 and over numbers 5 and 6; Pass the weaver B over the side-spoke four and under numbers 5 and 6 **(3)**. Bend weaver B over the three long spokes and weaver A behind them **(4)**.

Pass weaver B under the side-spokes 5 and 6, over number 4 then under the number 3. Weaver A passes over the side-spokes 5 and 6, under number 4 and over number 3 **(5)**.

1

Long

Travers

2

Z Z
X Y Y X
X Y Y X
Z Z

Variant

For a solid base you can double the side-spokes (see photo on the following page).

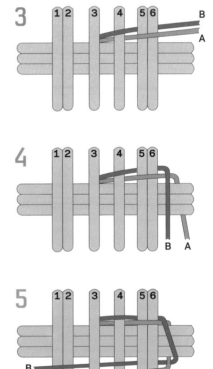

At the base of the slath, take two weavers, introduce them into the split in side-spoke 4 and use them to ligature the second half of the slath, working from right to left in the same manner as before **(6)**.

Do two more rounds, using weavers A and B on one half of the base and weavers C and D on the other. Bring the four weavers out on the underside of the base and cut them obliquely behind a spoke **(7)**.

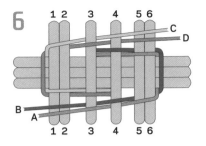

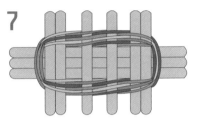

Breaking out

Bend the extremities of the long spokes and the side-spokes 1 and 6 outwards to from a star **(1)**.

Introduce a weaver under the side-spoke 2 and another under side-spoke 3 Pass weaver A over side-spoke 3, under number 4 and then bring it out. Pass weaver B over side-spoke 4 under number 5 and then bring it out **(2)**. Do a complete round interlacing the weavers in the same way **(3)**.

Start giving the base a slight convex shape (see "Note" on page 29). Then insert the weavers behind a spoke and cut them obliquely.

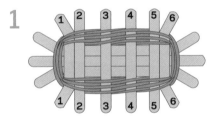

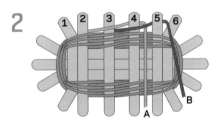

Filling

This is done in the same way as a round base slath (see pages 30-31).

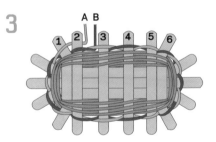

Peeling

Peel the base (see page 23).

With pruners, cut the spokes close to the weave to obtain the desired dimensions..

Variants

The slath can be made with more than three long-spokes, so it is possible to do the breaking out on two rounds: the first separates the long-spokes two by two **(1)**, the second round one by one **(2)**.

If you want a larger or rounder base insert a spoke on each angle on each round of breaking out, before starting filling **(3)**.

When the base is intended to be visible (a tray for example), you can decorate it using a selection of different weaves separated by a 3-strand wale (see pages 48-49).

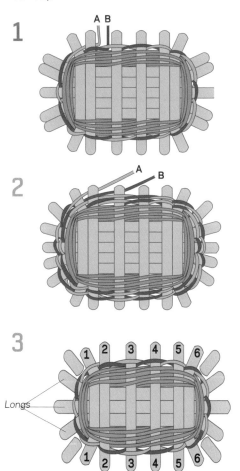

Square or rectangular base on framework

The framework

This is composed of spokes slightly longer than the base desired. Cut them from the strands put aside for this work (see page 22). Their number is proportional to the width of the base and they are spaced about three centimeters apart. Unless you intend to weave the stakes (see page 45), the outside spokes are joined two by two: these are the "banks" **(1)**.

It is essential to keep the frame in place during filling. Using two thick planks a little longer than the width of the frame and about 10cm high. Wedge the spokes between them as between the jaws of a vice **(2)**. Make sure the spokes are properly placed. Protect the bottom of the framework with a folded cloth and keep it firmly between your knees, or kneel on it.

Filling

This is done with a one-strand slew. Introduce a weaver under spoke one halfway up the length of the framework. Bend it over spoke 2, under spoke 3 and so forth to the bank on the right **(3)**.

1

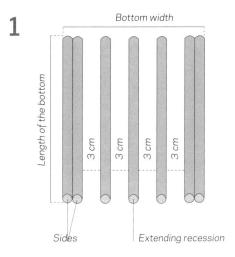

Bottom width

Length of the bottom

3 cm | 3 cm | 3 cm | 3 cm

Sides | Extending recession

2

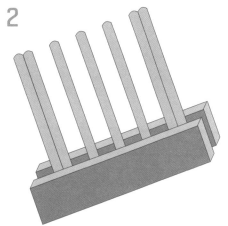

3

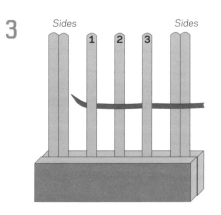

Sides | Sides

1 | 2 | 3

Variant

You can use finer spokes and double them (see photo on the next page).

38

Bend the weaver round the bank and then weave it from right to left **(4)**.

Continue to work progressing alternatively from left to right and right to left. Replace the weaver whenever necessary (see page 33). When the filling reaches the extremities of the spokes, bend the weaver round the left bank and cut it obliquely under spoke 1 **(5)**.

Pack down the filling with the rapping iron. To keep the weave in place do a round of pairing in the following manner: Bend a weaver in two around the left bank; weaver A will be on the base, weaver B under it **(6)**. Bring up weaver B. Pass weaver A under spoke 1 and then bring it up **(7)**. Pass weaver B over spoke 1, under spoke 2 and then bring it up **(8)**.

4
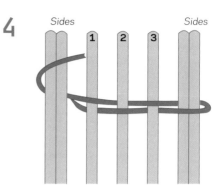

5
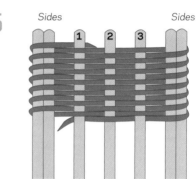

6
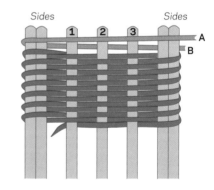

7
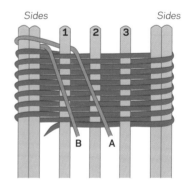

8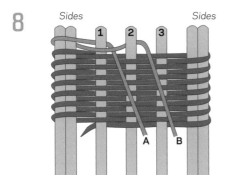

9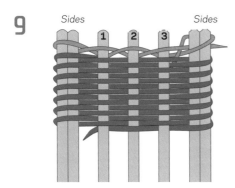

10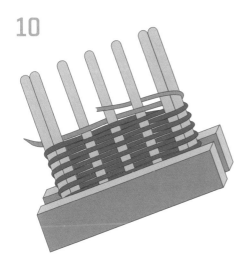

TWO-STRAND SLEW

It is also possible to fill in the base with a two-strand slew — working with two (or more) weavers side by side (see page 54).

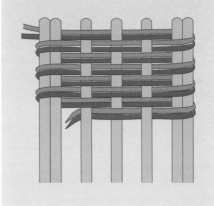

Continue to interlace the weavers in the same way. When you get to the end of the row, cut the under weaver obliquely under the right bank. Bend the second weaver round the right bank and bring it out. Now introduce it into the row of pairing and cut the end obliquely behind the last spoke **(9)**.

Protect the woven part of the framework with a folded cloth and place it between the two planks; now either grip it firmly between your knees or kneel on it. Introduce a weaver under the left bank and weave it in the same way as before to fill in the other half of the base **(10)**. Finish with a round of pairing.

Peeling

Peel the base (see page 23). With the pruners, cut the banks and the spokes close to the weave.

Base on a mould or frame

This method is used especially for making grids, but also for accessories where the perimeter mustn't get deformed, such as lids.

The mould or frame

Cut a strand at a length equal to the base's perimeter. Scarf the extremities (see page 23).

If you want a round or oval base, draw the outline on a board, put in a series of tacks about 3cm apart and then curve the strand inside the defined zone **(1)**. It is essential that the strand is sufficiently damp; if it is a rattan strand, you can make it suppler by heating it with a small blowtorch. Join the ends of the strand with two or three tacks, pushed in with flat pincers **(2)**, or by tying a splint around them **(3)**.

To make a square or rectangular frame, locate the places where the four angles will be by placing a split end in the center of the strand. Crush each angle with flat pincers then bend them **(4)**. Close the frame with tacks or splint.

The "heel" stakes

The heels are spaced at about 3cm on all the width of the mould or frame. Take the stakes reserved for this purpose and make a heel-cut at each end (see page 23). With a round or oval base the distance between the heels varies, as it should be equal to the base's length at the place where the heel will be woven **(5)**.

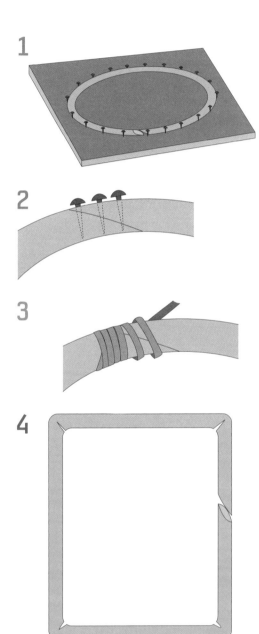

5

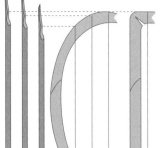

Starting with the first spoke, fit the heel onto the extreme left of the mould or frame, roll the thin end of the spoke round it, bring it from left to right in front of the heel then fold it down **(6)**.

Do the same to fix the spoke to the opposite end of the frame. Place the rest of the spokes in the same way from left to right, tucking the thin end of each spoke behind the one preceding it **(7)**.

Weaving the base

6

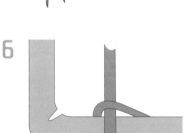

This is done by a one-strand slew. Introduce a weaver under the first heel-spoke, the weave in an over-under method, bending it round the mould or frame at the end of each row **(8)**. For a round or oval base start on the heel-spokes at the center and enlarge the rows little by little **(9).**

You can also use a two-strand slew (see page 41).

Once the base is filled in, cut the weaver obliquely, behind a heel-spoke.

7

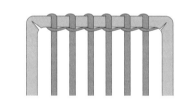

8

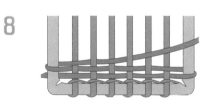

9

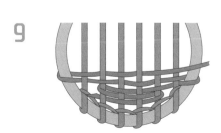

The stakes

Selected from the strands reserved for this purpose, the stakes form the skeleton around which the main body of the work is woven. Joining the stakes to the base can be done in two ways, depending on the type of base: by insertion or by weaving.

Inserted stakes

This method is fine for round or oval base slaths, and for square or rectangular bases made on a framework comprising double banks.

The general rule is to use one stake per spoke. Double this number if your material isn't very thick or if you want tidy, rounded forms.

Thin the ends of each stake (see page 23).

ROUND OR OVAL BASE

Place the base on a stool, the convex side face up. Introduce the awl parallel to one of the slath spokes in order to separate the pairing finish and the last rows of weave. Pull the awl out and push in a stake in its place. Continue in the same way, making sure that the stakes are introduced on the same side of the spokes **(1)**, or on each side if you are using double stakes **(2)**.

Press the blade of the pruning knife or pruners against a stake close to the paring edge and bend the stake upright **(3)**. Repeat this operation with all the stakes.

Tie the stakes loosely near the top with a splint or a piece of string to give the work the desired opening **(4)**.

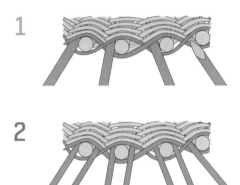

1

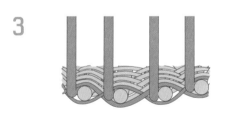

2

3

4

SQUARE OR RECTANGULAR BASE

Proceed along the two perpendicular sides as in a round or oval base. On the opposite side raise the weavers over the bank pairs with a awl and push in a stake horizontally, keeping the same space as those introduced beside the spokes.

Press the pruning knife blade or pruners close to the weave and bend the stake upright (**1**). Repeat the operation on each stake.

Keep the stakes in place at the desired opening by tying them with a splint or a piece of string (see fig. 4 on the previous page).

CORNERS AND POLES

When you want to reinforce a square or rectangular work, you can replace the four corner stakes with thick poles of rattan, wood or bamboo. Unlike ordinary stakes, corner poles must be cut to their final height before being put in place. Nail or staple the corner pole on the outer spoke of the bank (2) or thin one of its extremities and introduce it between the two banks through the row of pairing (3). It is also preferable to place a pole on both sides of each opening made in the work.

1

2

3

Woven stakes

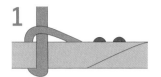

This method suits all bases made on a mould or a frame, as well as square and rectangular bases on a framework whose parallel sides are finished with a simple bank. Calculate the number of stakes by laying them all along the perimeter of the mould or frame or all along the framework banks; the space between each stake should be a little wider than their diameter. When you have chosen the strands, split them to make heel-stakes (see page 23).

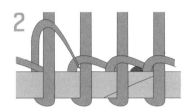

WEAVING ON A MOULD OR FRAME

Fit the heel-stake to the mould or frame, bend the thin part, bring it over the stake from left to right then bend it down behind the mould or frame (1).

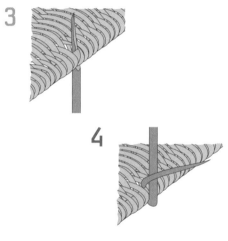

Proceed on the same way to weave the other heel stakes, working from left to right bending each thin end around the preceding stake to block it against the mould or frame.

Pass the thin end of the last stake under that of the first (2).

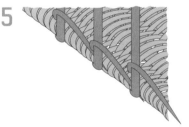

WEAVING ON A BANK

Insert the extremity of the first stake between two weavers, from bottom to top so that the thin end comes out on top (3). Stand the stake vertically and fit the heel against the outer bank then bring down the thin end in front from right to left (4). Weave the other stakes from left to right (5), spacing them regularly until you reach the other end of the bank (6).

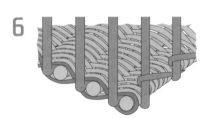

You can replace the stake at each corner with a corner-pole (see page 45).

Once the weave is finished, tie the stakes (see Fig. 4 page 44).

Placing stakes on a wooden frame or base

Wooden bases are smoother and easier to take care of than woven ones — which is an important quality for certain items, such as baskets used to hold foodstuff. In addition, they guarantee stability and correct dimensions, and make the work easier for beginners. You can use the wood of your choice, from simple plywood to elegant veneers or laminates, which have the advantage of being waterproof. The thickness (at least 5mm) should be adapted to the dimensions of the work.

Cut the wood to the desired size and shape. With a gimlet or a drill, make holes the same diameter as the chosen stakes, regularly spaced around the edge of the base, a few millimeters from the edge. Introduce the stakes, so that at least 20cm comes out on the underside **(1)**, and then create a simple border (see page 56) that will become the foot **(2)**.

If the material is supple enough, another method is to use one stake for two holes **(3)**.

Certain objects (drawers or racks for example) are made on 4D-frames **(4)**. For this, make a flat-cut on each end of the stakes (see page 23), to bend them at a 90° angle along the frame and then fix them with splint wound around the frame (see page 72-73), to hide the ends **(5 & 6)**.

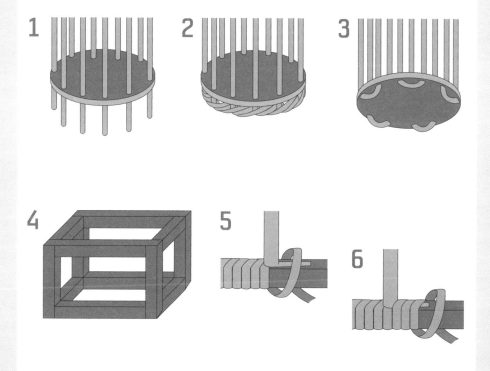

Upsetting

Upsetting makes the base and stakes more solid. This can be done on one round or several. Interlaced in the weave, it reinforces the weave and decorates it.

Upsett

Work with the weavers chosen for this method (see page 22). The height of the upsett depends on the solidity and the decorative effect desired. The stakes must remain parallel during the first two rounds, but you should pull them slightly outwards when weaving. If they have been inserted in pairs (one on each side of the base spoke) spread them while weaving to distribute them around the base. After two rounds, undo the string and start giving the object its shape (see page 52).

THREE-STRAND WALE BEHIND ONE STAKE

Introduce a weaver behind each of the first three stakes **(1)**. Pass weaver A in front of stakes 2 and 3, behind stake 4 and bring it out between spokes 4 and 5 **(2)**. Pass weaver B in front of two stakes, behind the next and bring it out between stakes 5 and six **(3)**. Proceed in the same way with weaver C to bring it out between stakes 6 and 7 **(4)**. Continue in the same manner.

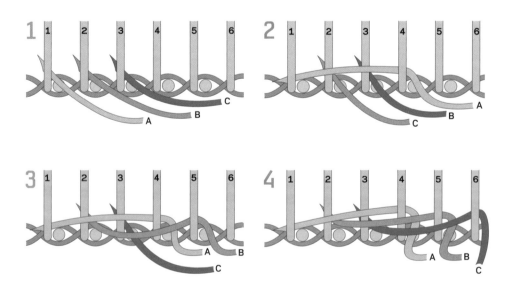

FOUR-STRAND WALE
BEHIND ONE STAKE

Introduce a weaver behind each of the first four stakes **(1)**. Weave them one after the other in front of three stakes and then behind the next **(2)**.

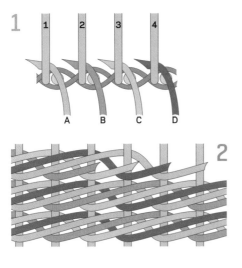

Single upsett

This is the same principle, but with only one round, so it must be done carefully. Each weaver must finish behind the stake where it was introduced **(1)**.

Overlapping two single upsetts behind a stake is called "fleur de lys" (lily flower), the first is done from left to right, the second from right to left **(2)**.

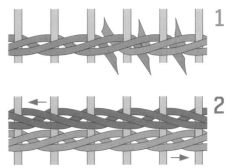

FOUR-STRAND WALE
BEHIND TWO STAKES

This gives the same aspect on both sides. Introduce a weaver behind each of the first four stakes. Weave them in front of two stakes and behind the next two.

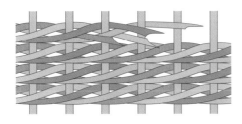

Common principles concerning upsetting

REPLACING THE WEAVERS
When the time comes to replace the weavers, do one last round and introduce the new weaver between the extremity of the old one and the following stake **(1)**.

FINISHING OFF
When the upsett reaches the desired height, bring the weavers out and cut each one obliquely in front of a stake with the pruners **(2)**.

HIDING THE SLATH SPOKES AND THE FRAMEWORK
Round or oval base slaths. The ends of the spokes are visible through the upset. If you want to add a foot to the base, its upper border will hide them (see page 62). If this isn't the case, there is a way of manipulating the spokes during the first round of upset to hide them. This technique will only work for a three-strand wale behind one stake where the stakes are inserted by pair.

Instead of introducing the weavers behind the stakes, insert them in the round of pairing that finished the base: place weaver A on the left of stake 1, the weaver B on the left of stake 2 and the weaver C on the left of stake 3 **(3)**. Pass weaver A in front of stakes 1 and 2, behind stake three and wedge it between this spoke and the next **(4)**. Weave weaver B normally making sure that it is placed under weaver A. Proceed with weaver C as with A **(5)**. Raise weaver A in a vertical position and bend it to the right in a way to pass in front of the next two stakes and the behind the following one. Do a complete round continuing to wedge the weavers when they come out between a stake and a spoke and then bending them on the next pass **(6)**.

Square or rectangular base on a framework. The ends of the spokes are visible on the two perpendicular sides. You can hide them before fixing the stakes of the opposite sides and eventually the corners.

With a small gimlet or a drill make two holes in the left spoke of each bank then introduce a weaver into each hole. Insert two other weavers into the pairing on each side of the other weavers. Pass the weaver A behind the first stake; pass weaver B in front of one stake and behind the other, the weaver C in front of two stakes and behind the following one and weaver D in front of two stakes and behind the following one **(7)**. Do a 4-strand wale behind one stake, then fix the weavers in the bank, as before **(8)**. Do the same work on the opposite side, then do an upsett of your choice around the perimeter of the work.

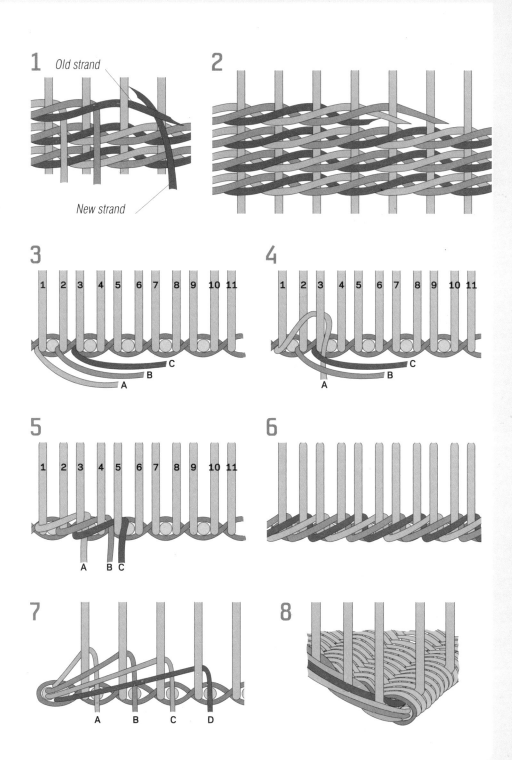

1 Old strand / New strand

2

3 1 2 3 4 5 6 7 8 9 10 11 — A B C

4 1 2 3 4 5 6 7 8 9 10 11 — A B C

5 1 2 3 4 5 6 7 8 9 10 11 — A B C

6

7 A B C D

8

The sides

This is the main body of the work, situated between the upsett at the base and the border at the top. You work by interlacing the weavers around the stakes. You can use different weaving methods to make the object more decorative.

Place the work on the stool; to keep the object stable while being able to turn it while working, put a weight inside it, or pin it with a awl pushed between the weavers of the base.

While you are working, thin the weavers (see page 23); introduce them and replace them according to the instructions on page 33. To obtain a good finish, the ends of all the weavers should be found inside the basket.

Shaping the object

You will start giving your object its definitive form on the third round of upsetting (if you have done more than two rounds), or on the first round of the sides, after tying the string or splint holding the stakes in place.

To obtain a cylinder, the stakes must always remain parallel, even if you pull them slightly towards you to pass the weaver. They should be parted towards the exterior if you want your work to have a wide mouth, or pushed towards the interior if not. Forming is done by pushing or pulling the stakes at each round. This operation needs to be regular and requires practice.

Using a mould makes this easier. For an oval or round object, make a mould (see page 42) of the diameter desired for the rim and fix it inside the stakes with a splint or a piece of string at the height you want to finish the work. If you are working on a square or rectangular item, tack two brackets in a cross on the stakes or on the corner poles.

Items are sometimes made from a full wooden shape, to which the bottom is fixed with metallic shafts, called "fine basketwork keys." When the opening of the object is narrower than the bottom, the shape is set by several parts that are removed when the work is finished. These forms can be replaced by a heavy object of an appropriate size.

ONE-STRAND SLEW

For this method you should have an odd number of stakes. If these are inserted stakes leave one out when they have been placed in pairs or add one if they have not. Introduce a weaver and proceed to pass it alternatively in front of and behind a stake.

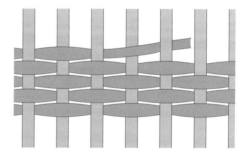

PAIRING (1)

Bend a weaver in two around a stake and weave alternatively in front of and behind a stake, interlacing the weavers.

TWO-STRAND SLEW (2)

This is the same principle as the one-strand slew (see page 52), but it is done with two or more weavers side by side. You must have an odd number of stakes for this method.

FRENCH RANDING

This is the most used method, especially when working with willow. It makes a dense and regular weave.

Prepare as many weavers as you have stakes; if they are long enough, you won't need to replace them. Introduce a weaver behind each stake, working from right to left **(4)**. Work the weavers one after the other in the order in which they were placed, from left to right, passing them alternatively in front of and behind a stake **(5)**.

If you are using thin material, it is possible to superimpose two weavers.

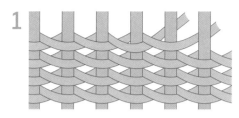

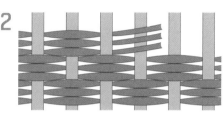

3-STRAND WALE (3)

Proceed in the same way as the upsett — with a 3-strand wale behind a stake (see page 48). You can also insert a single round in the sides made with another weaving method.

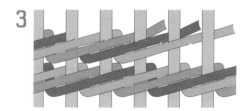

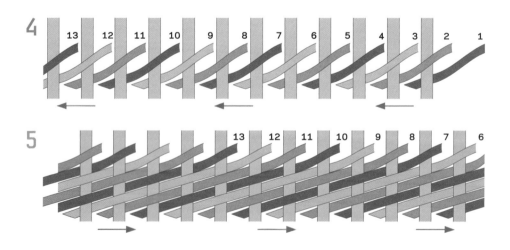

FOLLOWING WEAVERS

This method is particularly adapted for willow because it allows you to even out the variations in the thickness of the material due to its tapering diameter. Choose weavers equal to or longer than the perimeter of the work.

Introduce the first weaver behind stake 1 and pass it alternatively in front of and behind the stakes. When you get back to the starting point, leave it on the outside of the work **(1)**. Place the second weaver behind stake 2 and weave it in the same way **(2)**. Continue to work in the same manner, by introducing each new weaver behind the stake to the right **(3)**.

When the sides are finished, weave each tip over the foot of the following weaver **(4)**.

DAMASK

This method consists of working the weavers alternatively in front of two stakes and behind the two following stakes. You need an even number of stakes (on each side if your object is square or rectangular). The weavers pass either in front of or behind the corner-poles.

For French randing, introduce the weavers behind one stake out of two from right to left **(1)**, and then work them one after the other in the opposite direction **(2)**. If the weavers aren't long enough to reach the desired height, move them by two stakes to the right when you change them **(3)**.

It is also possible to work with following weavers as explained below **(4)**.

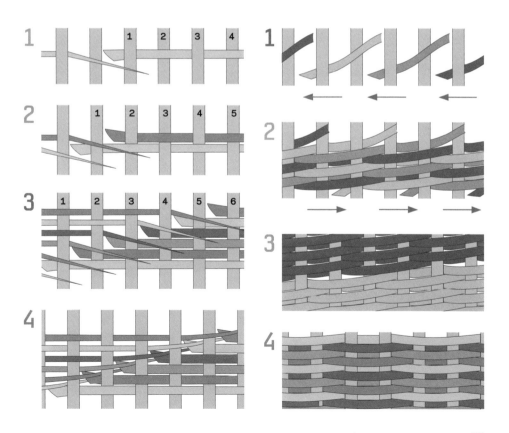

Borders

They finish off the top of your object and decorate it. This is done by weaving the stakes in a manner that turns them down progressively.

Simple border

The simplest method is achieved by "two stakes behind one."

Turn down spoke 1 behind spoke 2 and bring it out. Do the same with stake 2 and bring it out between stakes 3 and 4 **(1)**. Take up stake 1, pass it in front of stake 3, behind stake 4 and bring it out between stakes 4 and 5; it won't be used again **(2)**. Turn down stake 3 behind stake 4. Take up stake 2, pass it in front of stake 4, behind stake 5 and bring it out between stakes 5 and 6; it won't be used again **(3)**. Turn down and take up the rest of the stakes in the same way **(4)**.

If, at each pass you turn down a stake next to the one that has just been woven, you get a flat border **(5)**; if you place them above, you will have a raised border **(6).**

To finish off, interlace the last three stakes under the first two **(7 & 8)**.

Cut all the stakes obliquely close to the border.

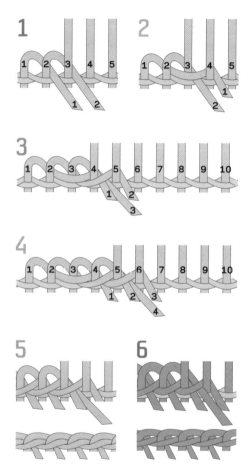

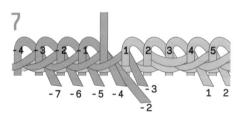

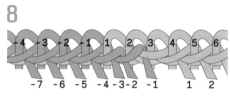

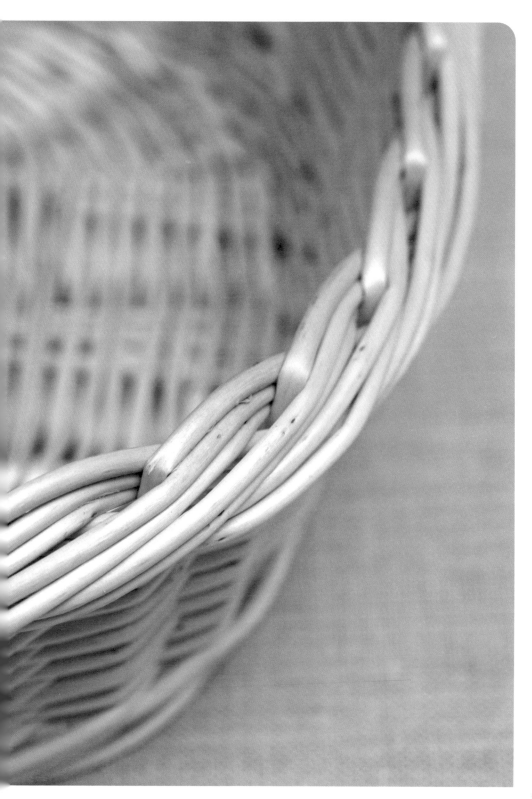

Variants

It is possible to create borders of three, four, five, or six stakes behind one. You should turn down the chosen number of stakes before taking up the first of them **(1 & 2)**.

Starting by turning down the chosen number of stakes you can also create a border behind two stakes **(3 & 4)**.

Double border

The simplest model is the "four stakes behind one" method. Use strands that are the same thickness as the stakes.

Insert a strand to the right of each of the first four stakes. Turn down the first three pairs of stakes behind the fourth stake and this last behind stake 5 **(1)**. Take up the first pair of stakes bend it behind stake 6 and bring it out **(2)**. Turn

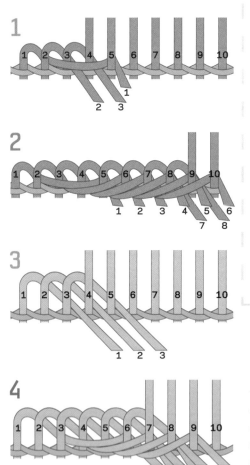

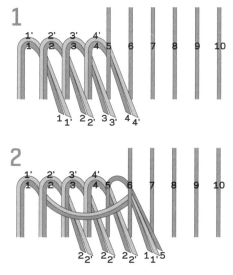

Rolled border

Take four strands the same thickness as the stakes. Insert two on the right of each of the first two stakes. Twist the first group of three stakes and bend behind the second group of three. Twist the second group and bend them behind stake three **(1)**. Leave one of the stakes of the twist 1 on the inside, twist stake three into the two remaining stakes, bend the new group in front of stake 4 and bring it out on the

stake 5 down behind stake 6. Take up the second pair of stakes and pass them in front of three stakes and behind the following one. Continue to work in the same way.

From stake 5 onwards you should have three stakes behind each stake: when it comes to taking them up, leave the bottom stake on the outside and only take the inside stake which has been turned down and the one immediately below it **(3)**.

Finish the border by weaving the last stakes under the first to keep the motive even **(4)**. Cut all the stakes obliquely close to the border.

As with simple borders, double borders can be created flat or raised and with different paces of rounds.

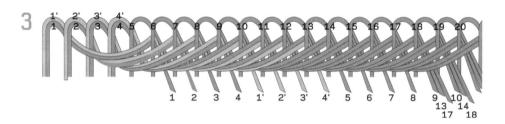

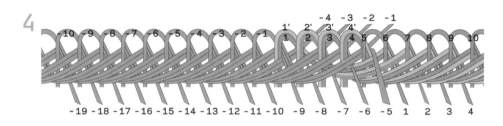

inside **(2)**. Continue to work in the same way all around the perimeter **(3)**. To finish pass the last stakes under the first **(4)**.

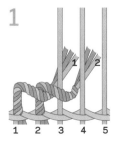

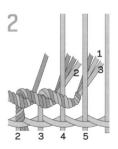

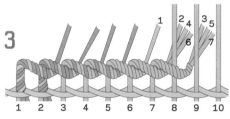

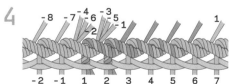

Braided border

Insert a pair of strands between stakes 1 and 2. Insert another pair to the left and turn them down towards the front. Place another in the same way **(1)**.

Weave pair C in front of two stakes and behind the next. Turn down stake 2 and pair A **(2)**. Weave pair B in front of two stakes and behind the next. Turn down the stake with the pair C; weave the pair A and the stake 2 **(3)**. Turn down stake 4 and pair B. Weave pair C and stake 3. Turn down stake 5 with stake 2 and one of the stakes from A; leave the other stake **(4)**.

Continue in the same way, leaving a stake each time you turn down one. Cut the ends of pairs B and C to be able to weave the last stakes which fit into the interior of the work **(5)**.

Border around a mould

This method can only be used for round or oval baskets. Make a mould of the same diameter as the opening (see page 42). Slip it onto the stakes and keep it firmly in place just above the sides. Pass stake 1 over the mould and insert it between stakes 4 and 5, bring it out entirely on the inside and then bring it out to the outside between stakes 5 and 6. Continue to work the other stakes in the same way.

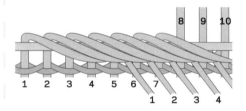

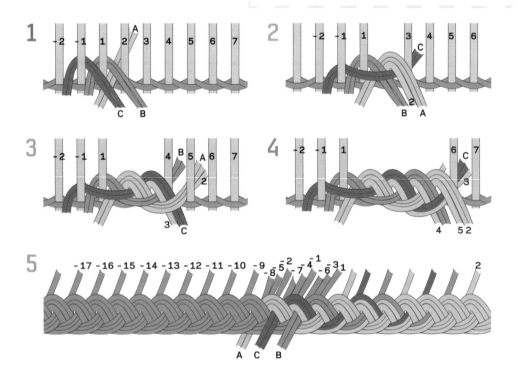

Corner-pole borders

Insert two strands just after the corner-pole on the right. Bend one of them around this pole in a way to bring it out to the exterior **(1)**. Create the border of your choice using this strand as a stake **(2)**. When you reach the second corner-pole, bend the last stake around it, insert it into the border and weave the second stake that you inserted under the first stake to the right **(3)**. Keep the weave in place with a twisted weaver (see the rule box on page 63) wound next to each corner-pole **(4)**.

Casings

If you want to add a fitted lid to your work, finish the sides with a single upsett, done with at least four weavers (see page 49). Turn down each stake according to the height desired for the casing — for example behind one, in front of one, behind one (narrow casing) **(1)**; behind two, in front of one, behind one, in front of one, behind one (higher casing **(2)**. Bring all the stakes out on the inside of the basket and cut each one obliquely behind the following one.

You can also make a casing on the lid so that it is the latter.

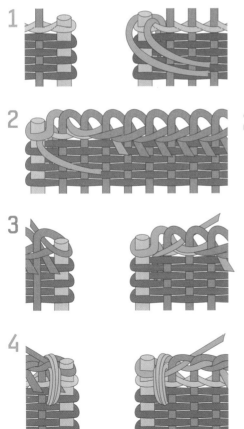

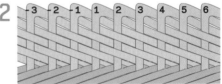

> ## Note
>
> Most of the time, the border is preceded by a round of pairing or an upsett. You can also make an open-weave border (see pages 80-81).

Finishing touches

Once the body of the work is finished, peel it carefully for the last time. You can then add the finishing touches of your choice: foot, handle, lid and fasteners.

Adding a foot

If you wish to raise your work's base, it is possible to add a foot.
Place the object upside down on the stool. Introduce a strand into the upsett next to each stake. Make an upsett until you reach the desired height (see pages 48-51) and finish with a simple border (see page 56).

Handles

SINGLE HANDLE
This method is for small handles, similar to those on washing baskets.
Calculate the length AB of the handle. Choose a thick strand and thin the ends (see page 23). Insert it into the border (B) and twist it along all its length. Insert it into border (A) and bring it out on the interior to form a "core" at the desired height **(1)**.

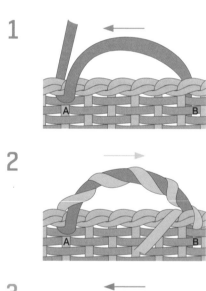

Bring it out to the front and twist it around the core. Insert it under the border to the right of core (B) and then bring it out to the left of (B) **(2)**. Bend it once more around the core from right to left and wedge it into the loop (A) formed at the beginning of the work **(3)**.

DOUBLE HANDLE

Thin the ends of a thick strand and a slimmer one (see page 23). Insert them into the border: the stake 1 in A, the stake 2 in B. Insert stake 2 into the border A and bring it out on the interior to form a core at the desired height **(4)**. Twist stake 1 and bend it around the core. Insert it under the border on the right of the core (B) and then bring it out on the left of B. Bend it around the core from right to left, pass it under the border (A) bend it around once

TWISTING A STAKE

When a stake must be twisted it is necessary to twist it beforehand to make it suppler. Insert one of the ends into the work to keep it in place, hold the other end between two fingers then exercise twisting movements from top to bottom.

again from left to right and then leave it on the exterior **(5)**. Twist stake 2 and bend it around the core from left to right. Introduce it under border (B) blocking stake 1 under it. Bend stake 2 once more from right to left and bring it out under the loop made by stake 1 **(6)**.

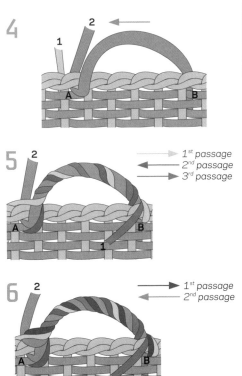

ALSATIAN HANDLE

For the core, thin both ends of a stake and insert them into the border on both sides of the basket.

Insert five stakes under the border on either the inside or the outside of the work, on the left of one of the ends of the core. Twist the stakes around the core. Repeat this operation on the other side with new stakes twisted around the core, doing this same number of rounds as before **(1)**.

At the base of each end of the handle make a cross-ligature (see pages 86-87) **(2)**, or bend one stake around the other four **(3)**. Cut the stakes obliquely.

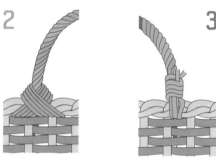

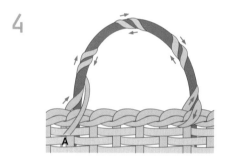

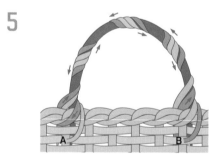

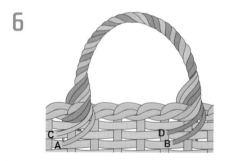

BIG BASKET HANDLE

For the core, thin both ends of a stake and insert them into the border on both sides of the basket.

Insert a first stake A under the border to the left of one end on the interior of the work. Bend it several times around the core. Insert it under the border from the exterior towards the interior and then bend it around the core again to bring it back to its starting point **(4)**. Repeat the operation with stake B inserted to the left of the other end of the core **(5)**, with stake C inserted to the right of A and then with stake D inserted to the right of stake B **(6)**.

It is important to always do the same number of rounds around the core. Insert the pairs of stakes under the border next to the two loops. Bring them out on the interior of the basket, wedge them under the loops situated at the base of the handle and cut them obliquely

TWISTED HANDLE

This handle is made before the border, above the sides finished by an upsett. Choose the four strands that will become the handle. Insert a stake on either side of each one. To make the core twist together the three stakes in group 1 and insert them in the upsett between groups 3 and 4 **(1)**. Twist the stakes of group 4 and twist them around the core. Repeat the operation with group 3 and then with group 2 **(2)**.

You can use the groups 1 and 2 to make a rolled border (see pages 58-59). If not insert the ends of all the stakes under the upsett, bring them out on the interior of the work, tuck them into the weaver and then cut them obliquely.

REINFORCED HANDLE

This solid, low-level model is intended to be fixed to a lid or to the sides of a hamper.

To make the core, thin one end of a stake and make a heel-cut in the other end (see page 23). Insert the stake into the weave, curve it **(3)**, fold it into a right angle on the inside and then weave it **(4)**. Once the core is in place, weave it in the same way as for a single **(5)** or double handle (see page 62-63).

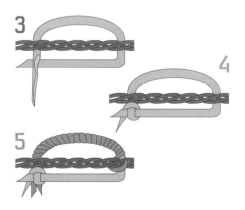

Lids

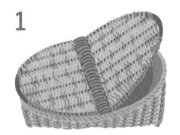

The shape and size of a lid should be identical to the opening of the basket. Lids can either be flat or have rims. In the second case, you just need to create a border with a casing. Casings are usually placed on the principal part of the work, but sometimes also on the rim of a lid (see page 61).

Round and oval lids

FLAT LID

Proceed in the same way as you did for making the base. If you choose the slath method, add spokes during filling to bring them closer together and to reinforce the lid. Finish by a round of pairing followed by a border.

LID WITH TWO FLAPS (1)

This should be made before the handle. For the central band, insert two stakes parallel into the border, in the middle of the basket and cover them with a one-strand slew (see page 52) **(2)**. Each flap is made in the same way as a base on a mould, around a stake that has been curved and held in place with a ligature **(3)**. Finish the one-strand slew with a simple border (see page 56) turning down the ends of the mould in the same way as the stakes. Fix the flaps to the central band with two or three hinges (see page 68).

LID WITH A RIM

Work on a slath. After the round of pairing, equalize the spokes on the edge of the weave and then insert the stakes (see page 44). Do a few rounds of 3-strand wale (see page 54) and then finish with a border.

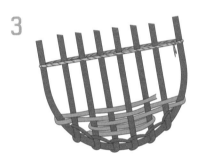

Square and rectangular lids

FLAT LID

Proceed in the same way as you did to make the base, working on a framework or a frame. In the first case, choose strands long enough so that they can be bent down when making the border and increase the number of stakes so that the lid will be more solid. If you are going to add a handle, join two thinner stakes in the center so that you can insert the handle's core between them. Finish the perpendicular sides of the banks by a round of pairing followed by a border.

If you want a lid with two flaps, you can create it either on a framework or on a frame (see glossary, page 92). When finished, fix them with hinges to the central band inserted in the center of the basket (see preceding page).

It is possible to leave indents on one side of the parallel stakes to eventually fix a fastener **(1)**. The banks opposite these slots are covered with a weaver inserted in the weave and rolled around them **(2)**.

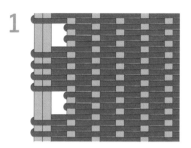

LID WITH A RIM

Work on a framework for this method. After the round of pairing, equalize the spokes, fix the stakes (see pages 44-46) and do a few rounds of 3-strand wale (see page 54) before finishing with a border.

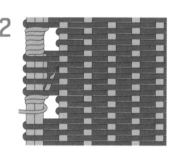

Hinges

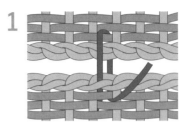

These are for turning a lid or a flap on the body of the work. They are placed at a few centimeters of each end and one or two others at the center when the item needing to be hinged is large.

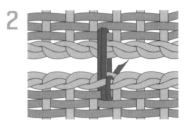

Place the lid on the basket. Insert a weaver in the main body's border, bring it out in the weave and twist it along its entire length. Insert it into the lid's weave and bring it out in the side of the main body (1). Repeat the operation a couple of times. Insert the weaver under the border of the main body, bring it out on the interior (2) and tuck it behind a couple of stakes.

Note

Working in the same way, you can also make leather hinges.

Closures

The most common system is made up of two clasps in relief, fixed upright to the main part of the work. They are fit into two long, flat clasps hung on the lid, then a shaft or a toggle slides between them.

Fasteners for the main body

Their height should be slightly more than the diameter of the shaft.

Twist a weaver along its entire length and bend it in half around a stake just under the border so that you can bring out the ends on the exterior of the basket **(1)**.

Twist the ends to make a loop then insert them a little lower on each side of the same stake **(2)**. Cross them over each other on the inside of the basket and tuck them under the loop formed in the beginning. Do a second fastener in the same way.

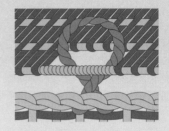

Fasteners for the lid

These should be long enough to encircle the fasteners on the main body. Twist a weaver along its entire length. Bend it in two around a stake just behind the border or the bank (if the lid is flat, or between the last round of weave if the lid has a rim).

Bring out the ends towards the exterior, twist them to make a loop then insert them on either side of the stake **(3)**. Cross the ends over each other on the interior of the lid and tuck them under the loop formed around the stake. Do a second fastener in the same way.

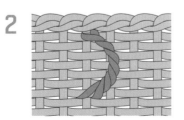

Peg

This is a straight, thick stick. If you want to make a ring at one end to stop it from slipping out of the fastener, thin one end, bend it in the shape of a ring **(1)** and then tie it down with a splint (see pages 72-73) **(2)**.

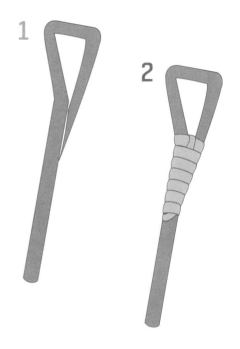

Affixing the peg

This is done in the same way as the shaft, but using shorter weavers. After thinning the two ends turn the weaver to form a half-circle. Thread the ring of the peg through one end. Insert the ends of the weaver vertically between the last round of weave and the border of the main body, to the right of the clasp, in a way that there is room for the peg to slip through the clasp when the lid-hasps are in place **(3)**. Cross the two ends of the weaver over each other on the inside of the basket and tuck them into the weave. Do the same thing for the fastener on the left, placing the curved weaver on the left side of the clasp.

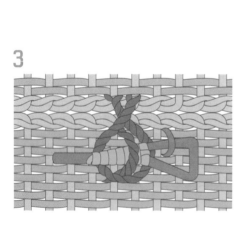

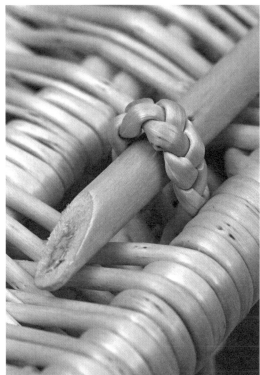

Use of splints

Any of the methods used for weaving the sides in closed-weave basketwork can be done using splints whatever the shape or the base of the work. The only conditions are: that the stakes are close together and that an upsett using stakes has been created at the base. You can also introduce a single or several rounds of three-strand wale from time to time while filling in the sides with splints. You can also fill in your base made on a slath of spokes, with splints placed flat.

Splints can be woven on their sides or flat between the stakes, with the sapwood uppermost. When you need to replace a splint that is on its side, overlap a new piece during the last two rounds **(1)**. If you are working on splints placed flat, simply leave the one that ends behind a stake and introduce the new one just after the stake **(2)**.

WRAPPING TECHNIQUES

Splints are used to cover accessories (handles, fasteners, rings) or wooden frames (see page 47). Align the end of the splint on the stake so that you can tuck it into the first rounds **(3)**. To finish lift the last rounds with a awl, insert the end of the splint through, bring it out towards the exterior **(4)** and cut it close to the wrapping.

SIDES AND BORDER MADE WITH SPLINTS ON ROUND STAKES

This procedure goes with any base created on a slath or on a framework. During every stage you can replace the quarters of split stakes by thick splints.

Split a thick stake in two at a length equal to the perimeter of the base. Make a mould or a frame with the quarters (see page 42) and then fit it around the base. Cut the stakes to their finished height, adding on a flat cut of a few centimeters at their ends (see page 23). Wedge them at regular intervals between the quarters of the mould **(5)**. Wrap a splint around the mould, fixing it to each spoke of the slath or framework with a stitch, 1 or 2 centimeters from the edge. If they are big enough, make a cut in the spokes and insert a splint into each cut **(6)**. If not pass the splint obliquely into the filling above each stake **(7)**. Fill in the sides with splints. Create a mould with two quarters and enclose the top of the stakes between them and cut them close to the mould. Wrap a splint around the mould, inserting a stitch on each stake **(8)**.

If you don't want to stitch the splints, make a flat cut into the top of each stake. A mould is placed above the sides and the flat cut is bent down against it. The splint is placed between the mould and the stakes and then wrapped around the flat cuts **(9)**.

At the base of the basket, wedge the ends of the stakes in the mould made of two quarters. Wrap a splint around the mould inserting stitches at regular intervals on the mould situated above **(10)**.

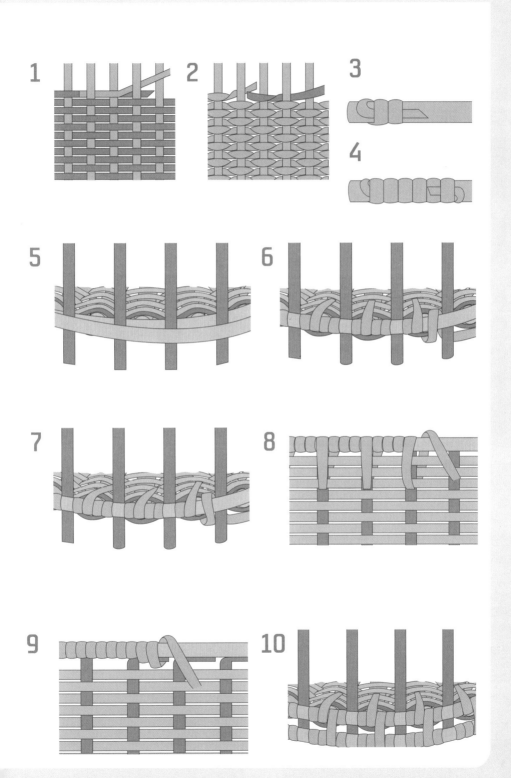

Open-weave basketwork

Items created with an open-weave have the same structure as closed-weave objects, but their stakes are visible and held together only by a few rounds of weave called "wale." This technique allows you to create light-weight items whose contents are visible and aired.

The open-weave basket technique allows you to create light-weight but solid items: clothes basket, handling baskets, bread and fruit stands, displays, etc. It is a very decorative technique also adapted to small items of furniture, table accessories and floral decoration.

Whether it is for aesthetic or practical reasons, you will often use closed-weave and open-weave successively while working on a single item. So that you can associate the two techniques and also anticipate the change from one to the other, make a sketch of the item you want to make. Jot down the dimensions and the principle characteristics, such as how you are going to do the base, the number of stakes, how you are going to do the upsett, the position of the handles, etc.

The base

This is always made in the same way, no matter what the form of your item. Make a mould or a frame in the dimensions you have chosen (see pages 42-43).

Prepare enough spokes to place them at intervals of one centimeter along the length of the mould or frame. Cut them a little longer than the base to allow yourself a margin for error when you are placing them.

The base wale

Choose a weaver long and rather thick. Bend it in two around the spoke on the left of the mould or frame, then bend the end A towards the front **(1)**.

Place a spoke perpendicular to the mould or frame on weaver B, bend weaver A to the right and bring out weaver B **(2)**.

Place a second spoke on weaver A and fix it by crossing the weavers as before.

Fix the following spokes in the same way. When the wale is finished, bend the two weavers around the spoke to the right of the mould or frame in the order that they present themselves and do several rounds from right to left **(3)**.

Do a wale at each end of the base. If it is big, place a sufficient number of spokes at regular intervals.

Start off with the one the closest to the center. If the base's dimensions are very large, do the wale with two weavers **(4)**.

1

2

3

4

5

WORKING POSITION

When you are working on the wale, the best position is to hold it with your knees. Place a wedge under the stool so that the front inclines upwards. Place the base on the stool with the front part extended out over the edge of the stool. Place a piece of wood covered with a cloth on the base, and hold it with your knee.

When the spokes are placed at a wide interval it would be better to do a meshed wale by twisting the two weavers around each other between spokes **(5)**.

Peel each weaver obliquely behind a spoke. Equalize the spokes flush with the mould or frame.

Stakes and bye-stakes

The body of an open-weave item is constituted of two sorts of strands: stakes which are used to form the border and bye-stakes which are cut just under it. If you are working with willow, its decreasing diameter means that the object risks being unequal. You should therefore cut the strands in half and use the top part as stakes and the bottom half as bye-stakes.

Stakes and bye-stakes are woven at regular intervals around the mould or frame (see page 46). As a general rule they are spaced at a distance slightly larger than their diameter. The thin end of the heel-cuts should be long enough to create a continuous border. Reinforce square and rectangular work by placing a corner-pole at each angle (see page 45).

To both hide the stakes at the base and to reinforce the item, you should create an upsett of a few centimeters at the bottom (see page 48). This also allows you to insert supplementary strands; these are the bye-stakes.

The wale

Do this exactly the same way as on the base (see pages 76-77), placing them a regular intervals on the height of the work.

CROSS-WORK

For this method you need an even number of stakes on the perimeter of a round or oval object, or on each side of a square or rectangular object. In this case the corner stakes should stay straight during the work.

Do a first round of wale keeping the stakes parallel, then do the second round, crossing the stakes two by two, always in the same direction **(1)**. If the operation is repeated during a third round, the stakes will return to their original position **(2)**.

1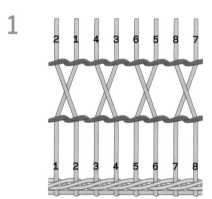

2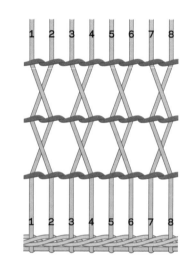

78

FANCY CROSS-WORK

To obtain a decorative lattice you can cross the stakes in different patterns **(3)**, modify the order of passage **(4)** or leave some of them vertical **(5)**.

Calculate the number of stakes you will need according to the pattern you want to achieve. For example you can do model number 4 with any even number of stakes, while models 3 and 5 need a multiple of six.

To get the correct number of stakes you can introduce bye-stakes into the upsett at the bottom of your object **(6)**. Know however, that you will need to keep them for the whole height of your work.

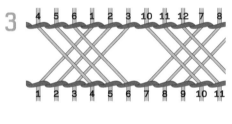

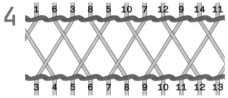

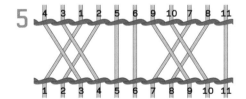

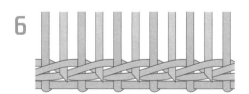

GIVING YOUR WORK ITS FORM

Because of its rigid structure, open-weave baskets have a constant angle between the base and the border. When you begin weaving, the stakes and bye-stakes should be firmly fixed, but in a way that makes titling them in the desired direction possible and in the amplitude which will be the object's opening.

Until the first round of wale is done, tie the stakes and bye-stakes to keep them from collapsing (see Fig. 4 on page 44). For a square or rectangular object, keep the corner stakes in place with a mould made from two sticks tacked or stapled in the form of a cross.

Another method consists of doing a wale by ligaturing the stakes two by two at the point where they cross **(7)**. According to the shape of your work and the pattern chosen, it is sometimes necessary to do a meshed wale to keep the stakes from getting too close together (see page 77).

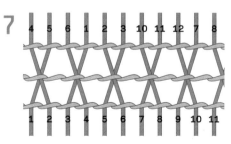

It is possible to insert an open weave in a closed-weave item, after doing a round of pairing or an upsett. The stakes can be left straight or crossed. In the second case you can do the wale with thin twine that can be removed once you have finished your basket Do another round of pairing or upsett and then continue your closed-weave **(8)**.

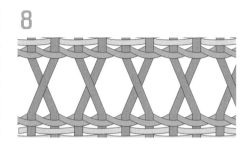

The border

Cut the bye-stakes close to the last wale. Do a few rounds of upsett (see page 48).

If there aren't enough stakes to do an interesting border, insert a stake into the upsett between each one. Bend a weaver around the first stake and weave in a pairing method (see page 54) to the fourth stake. Bring down the first stake to the front by bending it and introduce it into the last round of pairing **(1)** Continue in the same way for the following stakes. Bring up each stake by passing it under the following one **(2).** Repeat the operation but bringing each stake down under the following one **(3)**. Cut the stakes close to the border.

In the example number 3, each stake is brought down in front of the following two. You can modify the number to obtain different effects **(4 & 5)**

It is also possible to replace the scallops with picots by bending the stakes before bringing them down **(6)**.

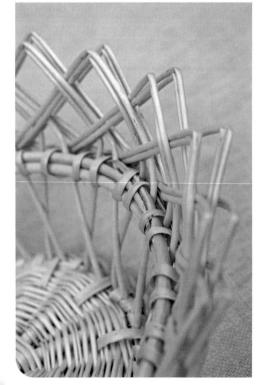

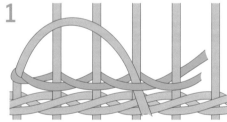

2

Variant

You can also create one or another of the borders explained in the chapter on closed-weave basketwork (see pages 56-61).

3

In front of two stakes

4

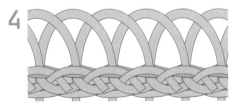

In front of three stakes

5

In front of one stake

6

Plaiting

This technique consists of creating the basket's volume by interlacing the weaver layers only, without resorting to the stakes.

Make a round or oval base slath. Choose very long weavers because they will be woven along the whole height of your basket and cannot be replaced during the work. Their number must be a multiple of eight for layers of four weavers, ten for layers of five weavers. Fix them around the base, between two quarter-stakes and held in place with a splint (see pages 72-73). Arrange them in groups of two layers, with a distance between each group of about equal to three times their diameter **(1)**. During the first round, cross the second layer of each group under the first layer of the following group, bringing this last to the left. Afterward, reverse the order of passing the layers at each round **(2)**. Bend a stake around the work, above the weave and the tie it with a splint, positioning the weavers vertically and spacing them regularly **(3)**. Block the weavers between two quarter-stakes and bend a splint around them to form a border **(4)**. Finish the foot as explained on page 72.

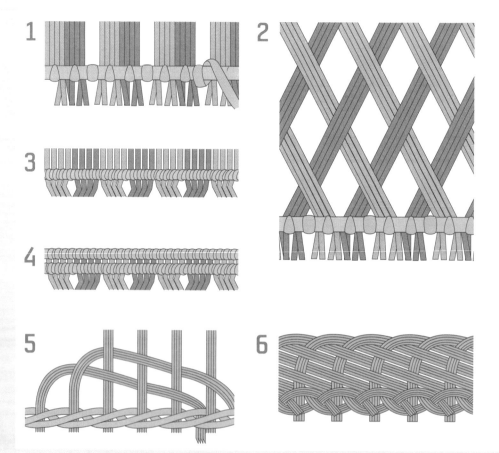

Laceries

This procedure calls for the layers of weavers woven without the help of stakes, and brought down in a way that forms the basket's border or its foot.

Make a round or oval base slath. Choose weavers long enough because it won't be possible to change them during the work. As a general rule four or five are used per layer. Insert them on each side of the slath's spokes (see page 44). The density of the lacery depends on the number of the weavers available. If you want to achieve a less open weave, replace the round of pairing, which finishes the base, with two or three rounds of a "three-strand wale behind one stake" upsett (see page 48): the space obtained between each weaver can receive a pair of extra weavers. Do a few rounds of upsett at the base of the weavers, spacing the latter carefully during each round so that they form flat, tight layers. Weave the layers one after the other, in a pattern of "in front of one, behind one," repeated as often as you wish, and then insert them into the upsett **(5)**. Interlace the last layers with the first, respecting the right order of passage.

Correct the layer's stiffness to obtain a regular result. A variant consists of not doing an upsett at the base of the basket and bringing out the layers towards the exterior and then weaving them the same way as the base of open-weave borders (see page 80) **(6)**.

It is also possible to create a flat lacery border around a base. In this case, the ends of the layers are brought out on the interior.

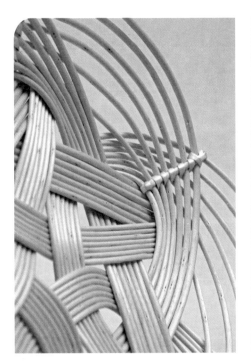

Rib basket weaving

Coming from an ancient agricultural tradition, this technique is sometimes called "rustic basketwork." The basket's shape is made on a carcass of solid ribs between which the weavers are interlaced.

Originally, rib baskets were made by peasants according to their agricultural or domestic needs. Made from tree or bush branches, they testified to a great practicality rather than to real craftsmanship. However, thanks to their solidity and rustic charm, these pieces have their own special place in the world of basketry.

Rib work baskets have a thick weave, rather like closed-weave baskets, but they are noticeably different with the swell of their ribs and by the particular pattern that forms the handles.

The carcass

This is made with two round or oval moulds, set one into the other. Placed horizontally, the first delimits the opening of the basket; the second placed vertically serves as the base and the handle.

With two thick strands (see page 22) make two moulds of the dimensions of your choice (see page 42). Place mould A into mould B making sure that they are correctly centered **(1)**.

The two moulds are fixed in place with a cross-ligature. Place a weaver behind one of the intersections of the two moulds. Bring it out in corner 1, re-insert it in corner 3, pass it over its end to block it and then bring it into corner 4 **(2)**.

Pass the weaver over and into corner 2, bring it out again in corner 3 and then pass it over the lower stake of mould B **(3)**.

Pass the weaver around the left stake of mould A, from front to back **(4)**.

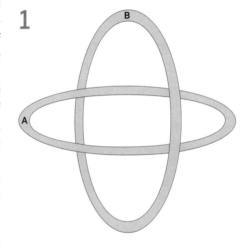

Do a few rounds, weaving on the three carcass stakes **(5)**.

Repeat the operation on the other side of the basket.

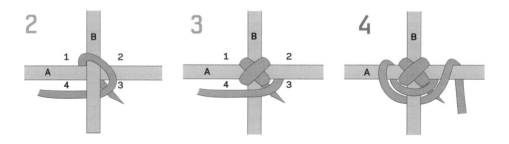

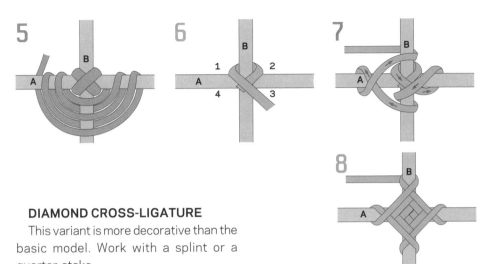

DIAMOND CROSS-LIGATURE

This variant is more decorative than the basic model. Work with a splint or a quarter-stake.

Place the splint in front of the intersection of the two moulds on a slant from corner 4 to corner 2. Pass it behind the upper stake of mould B and bring it over into corner 3 **(6)**.

Pass the splint around the right hand stake of mould A (from bottom to top), around the lower stake of mould B (from left to right), around the left hand stake of mould A (from top to bottom) and then around the upper stake of mould B (from right to left) **(7)**. Repeat this until the cross-ligature is large enough **(8)**.

Working in the same way as the basic model, weave several rounds of one-strand slew with a weaver and then do the other side in the same way.

Proceed in the same way as the basic model to place the ribs and weave the sides.

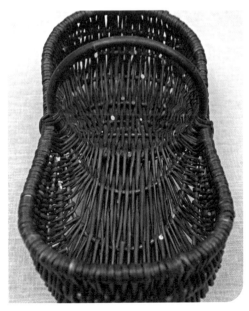

The ribs

In addition to the carcass, which decides the volume, the skeleton of the basket has ribs. The number, their size, and their arrangement vary according to the shape you want to give your work. The sketches below analyze the structure of four classic models. Cut pairs of stakes to precisely match the length of the desired shape. Thin each end and then bend them.

PYRENEAN AND GRAPE-PICKER

The carcass of the Pyrenean consists of two moulds set one into the other at a right angle, the vertical one serves as the handle. Two cross-ligatures are done on the intersections, in the center of the basket's large sides. Made in the same way the grape-picker has rounded sides.

TOSCA

This name regroups all the models whose carcass is made of one mould to delimit the opening and ribs placed lengthwise. The cross-ligatures are done on the short sides to fix the mould and the central rib placed perpendicularly to it. The handle, big basket handle or Alsatian (see page 64) is added on the larger sides.

FLAT-BACKED BASKET

The carcass is made with an oval mould whose upper part serves as the handle, set into a semi-circular mould which delimits the opening. The ribs of the back are placed flat and inserted according to the progress of the sides.

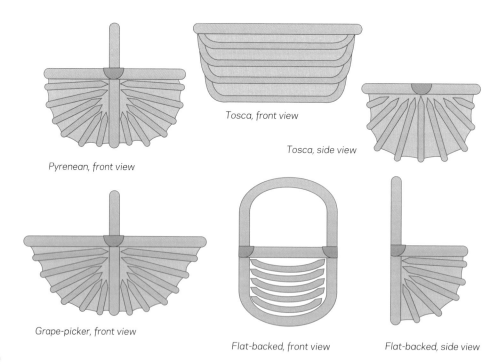

Pyrenean, front view

Tosca, front view

Tosca, side view

Grape-picker, front view

Flat-backed, front view

Flat-backed, side view

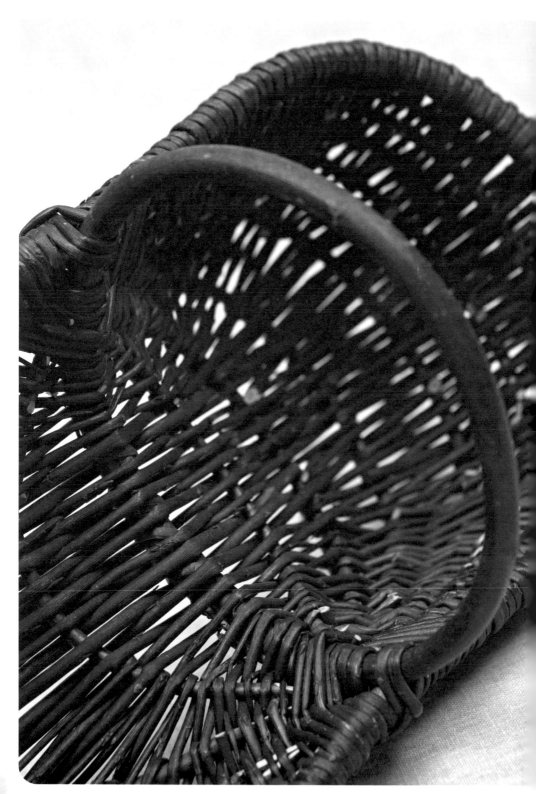

The weavers

Insert three ribs on each side of the vertical mould by wedging their ends into the cross-ligature **(1)**.

Work with a one-strand slew (see page 31) on one of the sides of the basket. To keep the weave from slipping, you will need to do a "dead round" at the beginning and at the end of each row, by bending a weaver once around the horizontal mould before going on with the weave **(2)**. After a few rounds, insert two more pairs of ribs into the weave **(3)**.

Continue to work as before until you reach the center of the basket's base.

Do the same for the other side of the work so that the two halves of the sides join. You can leave the handle as it is or cover it with a twisted weaver or a splint.

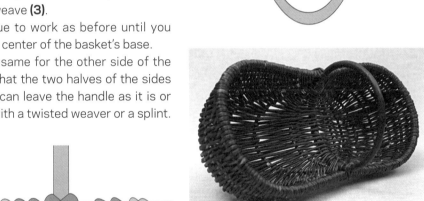

2

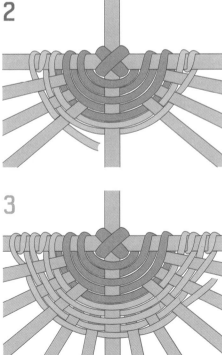

3

Glossary

Awl. Tool used for parting the weave.

Banks. Spokes that are joined on the sides of a framework.

Base. The bottom of the basket which, either flat or convex, assures its stability.

Bending. A technique that consists of wrapping a splint around a stake to hide it, or to join stakes.

Border. The weave at the top of a basket.

Breaking out. Round of weaving that serves to separate the slath spokes.

Buff. Willow peeled after boiling, which gives it a reddish color.

Bye-stakes. 1. In open-weave basket work, these are stakes that are not part of making the border. 2. Stakes that are inserted into the upset in open-weave basketwork.

Cleave. A three or four edged boxwood tool used for splitting

Core. Center of a handle.

Corner-poles. Stakes of a large diameter placed in the corners.

Crocane or French randing. A weaving method using one weaver per stake or per spoke.

Cross-ligature. Ligature used to fix ribs or handles.

Damask. Method of weaving presenting vertical bands.

Dead round. Bending a weaver around a stake, a spoke or a rib situated at the extremity of a row.

Enamel. Term used to describe the brilliance of a strip of rattan.

Esparto. Making items using vegetable fibers that are braided or spiral.

Filling. Weaving the spokes of a slath or framework.

Fine basketwork keys. Small metal stems used to fix the base of a basket onto a wooden base.

Fleur de lys. Superimposing two single upsetts in opposite directions.

Foot. 1. The thickest end of a willow strand. 2. Upsett added to the base of a basket.

Form. Forming is done by pushing the stakes towards the interior or pulling them towards the exterior while weaving the sides, to determine the diameter of the opening.

Frame. Square or rectangular mould.

Framework. All the stakes around which a square or rectangular base is woven.

Heel-cut. A type of cut in the form of a heel made in the end of a strand that has been split so that it can be woven.

Hollows. Stakes that make up the framework of a square or rectangular base.

Husking, or Stripping. Operation consisting of removing the bark from a strand.

Lacery. Technique that consists of interlacing layers of weavers without stakes to form a decorative border or foot.

Ligature. A weaving method to tie a round or oval base slath.

Long. The spokes placed lengthwise in a round or oval base slath.

Mould. Curved stake whose ends are joined to form a round or oval structure.

Pairing. Weaving method using two weavers that cross at each stake of spoke.

Passage. Movement of a weaver around a number of stakes according to the weaving method used.

Peeling. Operation that consists of cutting the stakes close to the work.

Peeler. Knife used for peeling.

Planes. According to their model, they are used for making splints.

Poles. Strands with a large diameter placed here and there in the basket.

Quarter stakes. A stake that has been split into three or four along its length, using a cleave.

Rapping iron. A tool used for packing in the weave after each round.

Reed gauge. Small ruler used to measure the thickness of rattan core strands.

Ribs. Stakes that make up the skeleton of a rib basket.

Round. Row of weave done around the perimeter of the basket in a way so that it comes back to its starting point.

Row. Passages done from one end to the other of a flat piece of work.

Sap-wood. Part of a strand found just under the bark.

Scarfing. Bevel practiced in both extremities of a strand then superimposed to join them to make a mould.

Shave. Plane for thinning the width of the willow.

Sides. Main body of the basket between the upsett and the border.

Side-spokes. In a round or oval base slath, the spokes that are laid across the width.

Single upsett. An upsett done on a single round.

Slath. A collection of spokes around which the round or oval base is woven in closed-weave basketwork.

Soaking. Operation consisting of immersing the vegetable fibers in water so that they become supple before using them.

Splint. Thin strip of willow cut from the sap-wood or from the bark.

Splitting. 1. Dividing a strand into quarters. 2. Cutting the end of a stake.

Spokes. 1. Thick strands. 2. Strands that form a slath or a framework.

Spokeshave. Small plane for thinning strands.

Stick. Large strands of willow used for making feet.

Stitching. Ligature done to assemble two pieces during bending.

Strand. General term for a vegetable branch used in basketwork.

Strip. A thin band of rattan.

Sweating. Keep the strands wrapped in a damp cloth to keep them supple after soaking.

Tank. Vat of water used to preserve willow strands to provoke re-vegetation.

Thinning. Cut practiced on the end of a strand to thin it.

Three-strand wale. Weaving method used in the sides, employing the same technique as the upsett — three weavers behind a stake.

Top. The thin end of a willow strand.

Two-strand slew. Weaving method done with a layer of two or more weavers.

Upright stakes. Stakes fixed perpendicular around the base to serve as the skeleton of the basket.

Upright shave. For making splint from the length of the willow.

Upsett. Weaving method done with at least three weavers. It is always placed at the base of the work and is also done to reinforce any part of the basket (for example under the border) or for a decorative effect.

Wale. In basketwork, a round or a row of weaving done in regular intervals to fix the spokes of the base, the stakes or bye-stakes in open-weave basketwork.

Weave. Fixing a split stake with a heel-cut to a bank, a mould or a frame.

Weaver's pruning knife. Tool used to split strands.

Weavers. Strands used in weaving the sides.

Willow brake. Tool used for stripping willow.

Wooden base. Wooden structure rather than a woven base, around which supple material is woven.

Acknowledgements:
The author and the editor wish to express their thanks to:
Vincent Reyntjens for passing on his knowledge and to Claude-Marie Reyntjens for her kindness and support; to Franck Douineau* for his enthusiasm and the relevance of his instructions; and to Jérôme Maillard* for his precious information.

We would also like to thank:
The Villaines-les-Rochers' Cooperative* for its friendly welcome and for supplying the necessary materials used to realize all the photos; and Mr and Mrs Szepes* for their excellent advice.

Originally printed in France by IME.
© Fleurus Editions, 2010
Registration of copyright: March 2010
ISBN: 978-2-215-10148-2
MDS code: 591234
1st edition N° P10024

Editorial management: Christophe Savouré
Edition: Agnès Busière and Marion Dahyot
Artistic direction: Laurent Quellet and Julie Pauwels
Photos: Jérôme Pallé
Sketches: Marie Pieroni
Fabrication: Anne Floutier and Thierry Dubus

Notes